W9-BAX-093

SECURITY!

SECURITY!

How to Protect Yourself, Your Home, Your Office, and Your Car

by Martin Clifford

DRAKE PUBLISHERS INC

NEW YORK

Published in 1974 by
Drake Publishers Inc.
381 Park Avenue South
New York, New York 10016

© Martin Clifford, 1974

Library of Congress Cataloging in Publication Data

Clifford, Martin, 1910–
  Security! How to protect yourself, your home, your
office, and your car.
  1. Crime prevention. 2. Industry—Security
measures. I. Title.
HV7431.C56   643   73–18067
ISBN 0–87749–600–5

Printed in the United States of America

Contents

Chapter 1. The No-Cost, Commonsense Approach
  To Security   1

Chapter 2. How to Make Your Home More Secure   9
    How Not to Cooperate with the Burglar   15
    What to Do if You Have Been "Burgled"   23
    What Should You Do in an Emergency?   25
    Viewer vs. Chain   27

Chapter 3. Locks and Alarm Systems   29
    Specialty Locks   34
    Who Are the Burglars?   35
    Break-in Types   37
    Forms of Protection   40
    How Simple Alarm Systems Work   43
    Circuit-System Advantages and Disadvantages   50
    Magnetic Switches   57
    Electronic vs. Electrical Systems   60
    Photoelectric Burglar Alarms   62
    The Capacity Alarm   64
    Sound and Vibration Alarms   65
    Ultrasonic Alarms   65
    Combined Protection   68
    Where to Put the Sensor Switches   68
    Alarm Timing   73
    Police Alarm   73
    How to Position Intruder Alarms   74
    Don'ts of Intruder Alarm Installations   75
    The Add-On System   76
    The Lock Alarm   77
    Window Jammers   77
    The Alarm   79
    Simple Door or Window Alarms   80
    Tha Alarm Problem   83
    Horn Ratings   83
    The Alarm Battery   84

Chapter 4. Bunco   87

   Pigeon Drop   88

   Jamaican Switch   91

   Mexican Charity Switch   93

   Jamaican Trust Game   95

   Paddy Hustle   96

   Creepers   98

   The Badger Game   98

   Marriage Bunco   100

   The Moneymaking Machine   101

   Short-Change Artists   103

   Bunco Crimes Involving Police Impersonations   104

     1. The Abortion Shake   104

     2. The Bookmaker Shake   105

     3. The Badger Game Shake   105

     4. The Fruit Shake   105

     5. The Till Tap   107

   Pickpockets and Purse Picks   108

   How to Protect Yourself Against Pickpockets   109

   Gypsies   111

   The Williamsons   112

   Magazine Solicitors   113

   The Religious Bunco   114

   Your Self-Protection   115

   The Lemon Game   117

   Phony-Bank-Examiner Shake   119

   Gold-Sale Bunco   122

   Coupon-Book-Sales MO   123

   Store Taps   126

Chapter 5. How to Protect Your Apartment   127

   Dogs in Apartments   134

   Apartment Lighting   136

   Your Front Doorbell   137

   More About Locks   138

   Tamper-Proof Cover   139

   Using the Services of a Locksmith   140

   Special Locks   140

   Your Key Ring   141

   Your Insurance   141

Chapter 6. How to Make Your Car More Secure   143
    Stealing to Order   145
    The Opportunity Thief   147
    The "Car-Parts" Thief   148
    The Joyrider   148
    The Vandal   149
    How to Protect Your Car   150
    Anti-Theft Accessories   154
      Interior Knobs   155
      Wheel Locks   155
      Battery Lock   156
      Hood Lock   157
      Steering-Wheel Lock   157
      Tape-Deck Lock   157
      Ignition Switch   158
    Car-Equipped or Self-Equipped?   159
    Auto Alarms   160
    Siren Recycler   162
    When to Protect Yourself   165
    Car-Parking Check List   165
    Protecting Your Gasoline Supply   166
    Temporarily or Permanently Stolen?   167
    The Warning Alarm Sticker   167
    The Time-Delay Protector   169
    Your Other Vehicles   169
      How to Protect Your Motorcycle   169
      How to Protect Your Bicycle   170
      Bicycle Anti-Theft Check List   173
    Insurance   174

Chapter 7. Security in the Office   175
    Building Security   176
    Protecting the Office   177
    The Three Steps to Office Security   178
    Telephone Larceny   180
    Insurance   180
    Personnel   180
    The Office Check List   181

Chapter 8. Travel Security   183
    Eyeball-to-Eyeball Confrontation   186
    Judo and Karate   187
    Hotel Theft   187
    Losing Your Luggage   188
    Your Credit Cards   189
    Car Pooling   190
    Watching Your Luggage   191
    Sleeping and Theft   191
    Check List for Traveling Security   192

Chapter 9. Miscellaneous Security Information   201
    Self-Protection   203
    The Sex Criminal   204
    Body Alarm System   206
    Using a Gun   207
    Installing a Home-Protection System   209
    Places of Entry   209
    Damage to Your Home   210
    The Victims of the Offense   211
    The Burglar's Tools   212
    Subterfuge Techniques   212
    The Telephone-Call Trick   213
    The Inspectors   213

Glossary   215

Chapter 1

The No-cost, Commonsense Approach to Security

There is no such thing as absolute security since we must work with, live with, and associate with people. Man is a social animal, but sometimes he is a bit more animal than social. There are many things you can do to protect your person and your property, and interestingly, these many things do not always involve the purchase and installation of protective equipment.

Crime is like death. We are, all of us, reluctant to admit it can happen to us. And yet it can not only happen, but often does happen because we are so cooperative with those who want to rob, maim, or kill us. To be as free as possible of a crime against you means you must take an important first step, and that essential step is awareness. Call it crime-conscious-ness, if you like, or alertness, or anything else. The fact is that if you have a realization of the possibility of crime, then you have taken a forward move to eliminate or to minimize it.

Many crime-prevention techniques are based on such awareness. If you are going to park your car on the street, select, if possible, a location under a bright street lamp. Close
the windows of the car, latch the side windows, and make
sure the doors are locked. Don't take for granted that slamming
the door of a car will automatically lock it. It may or may not.
Try the doors—not just the one you used, but all of them. Don't
leave anything of value out on a seat where it can be seen;
and don't try to cover merchandise or personal items with a
blanket or newspapers. These possessions, plus any suitcases,
should be stored in the trunk, and smaller items in the glove
compartment. Valuable electronic equipment such as a CB
unit, cartridge player, etc., are fair game for any thief who spots
them through your car window. Use an auto alarm and make
sure it is set before you leave the car. Affix a side window
sticker emphasizing that your car is burglar-proofed.

Will all of these steps guarantee your car against theft?

No, they won't do that, but they will increase the odds in your
favor, and that is about the best you can hope for. The important point here is that awareness has made you less susceptible to becoming still one more crime statistic.

This concept of awareness applies to everything you own
—your car, your home, and more important, to your own person. If you must walk down a deserted street, follow the most
lighted path; keep away from doorways and empty lots. If you
must walk through a high crime area in the daytime, even
with people out on the streets, take certain precautions before
you do so. Don't keep your wallet in your hip pocket or a pants
pocket. Put it in your jacket breast pocket. And make sure that
breast pocket is a deep one. When you buy a suit, check the
breast pocket to make sure it extends at least one inch—preferably more—above the top level of your wallet. If not, have
your tailor alter the pocket. Avoid small wallets that form a
bulge. A bulge in your breast pocket is an advertisement.

Of course, these are all commonsense suggestions, but then
common sense isn't quite as widespread as you might imagine.
All of these things—avoiding a bulging pocket, locking car

doors, and parking under lights—are simply a part of aware-ness. Your safety and security are dependent in great part on the constant and conscious effort you make to protect yourself and your property.

For some thieves, anything you have and anything that can be resold are suitable targets. Wallets and pocketbooks are preferred since these may contain cash and credit cards. They may also hold house keys and car keys, plus personal identifi-cation. With your keys and your address, it doesn't take a very imaginative thief to realize he has entrée to your home and your car. If you carry a pocketbook, keep your keys on a key ring or in a key holder without any form of identification. If you use credit cards have at home a record of the account numbers, and notify the credit-card company immediately if you lose your cards.

Obviously, you are going to carry some money in your wallet or pocketbook. There are two things you must do as far as pocketbooks are concerned: (1) Make it as difficult as possi-ble for a pickpocket to get into it; and (2) make it as difficult as possible for someone to snatch the pocketbook from you. Avoid pocketbooks that depend on friction closing. If you can open the pocketbook with a flick of your fingers, so can a thief. Get a pocketbook with a positive-locking type closure, pref-erably one that requires a sliding movement in two directions. That isn't all, though. That pocketbook should have a pocket with a zipper, and the longer the zipper the better. Inside that zippered pocket you should have a change purse, but make sure that the change purse has a lock that can't be opened with one finger. Now, that's a lot of trouble and inconvenience for you when you want to get at your money, but if it is difficult for you (and you are familiar with your pocketbook) think of how much more troublesome it will be for a pickpocket.

Not all thieves have pickpocket skill. Some of them depend on snatch and run. This involves a number of stealing tech-niques. Some thieves prefer cutting .the shoulder straps of your bag, and they can do this and be off and running with it before you have recovered from your shock long enough to scream. The solution is to make sure the shoulder strap is as strong as possible. Some leatherette straps are so thin and flimsy they can be cut with a cuticle scissor. A metal pocketbook strap is best; if unavailable, get one that is multiple-stranded.

The safest way to carry a pocketbook is with the strap on the shoulder opposite the pocketbook. This means your head and part of your body are covered by the straps. If you carry your purse in your hand, it can be snatched with a force and vigor that will leave you speechless. If you must carry your pocketbook, at least twist the strap around your arm several times. You can be sure the thief isn't going to snatch just any purse. He is going to take the line of least resistance and make off with the pocketbook that offers the greatest chance of success.

A wallet has a better chance for survival, and as mentioned earlier, is best carried in a breast pocket. An easy form of protection is to use a zipper across the top of the pocket. The zipper cannot be seen and does not affect the wearability of the garment. For best security, do not use the "straight-across" kind of zipper. Instead, get one that goes across and then turns down at a right angle for about one inch or so. You can, as a temporary expedient, use a safety pin. Two pins are better. Yes, it does sound silly to tie yourself up with "diaper pins," but losing your wallet to a pickpocket does indicate he is more security-conscious and alert than you are.

Ladies' hats, and men's hatwear, particularly the more expensive types, can be and are stolen. A mink hat is a tempting item. The only way you can protect expensive headgear is not to wear it in very crowded areas, or in high-crime areas. This doesn't mean the hat won't be stolen—just that you have become security-conscious and are trying to improve the odds somewhat.

Next to wallets and pocketbooks, jewelry offers an enticing target. If you must wear a diamond ring, make sure it fits and that you wear guard rings with it. Wear valuable pendants, earrings, rings, brooches, or pins only in safe areas. No restaurant is a safe area, no matter how well it is lighted or attended. No theater is a safe area. No public place is a safe area. Any excessive display of jewelry attracts attention, and once that happens you may be selected and followed. Security means being conscious of possible trouble, anticipating it, and doing everything you can to avoid it.

There is no place where security isn't important. If you are on a subway, select that car used by the conductor for opening and closing the doors. This means you should avoid the first and last cars, and stay somewhere toward the center. If you must go on a subway or train platform at night, don't do so unless the platform is occupied by people. Stay where people are. Avoid subway and train passageways that are empty and dimly lit. Try to schedule your traveling so that you avoid very late night hours, if possible. Bus and train terminals can be areas of personal danger during those times when "people traffic" is light or practically nonexistent. If your work schedule is such that it involves night travel, consider whether your life and property are worth the risks you must take.

Because murder, rape, robbery, and aggravated assault always seem to happen to someone else, consider that throughout the country:

- There is a burglary every 29 seconds.
- There is a robbery every 4 minutes.
- There is a forcible rape every 22 minutes.
- There is one murder every 56 minutes.
- There is an aggravated assault every 2¼ minutes.
- In one year (1972) over 2 million homes and apartments were burglarized.
- In that same year, over 720 million dollars in property and personal goods were stolen.
- Only one out of every five burglars is forced to stand trial.
- Residential burglaries have increased 334 percent in the last 10 years.

You should view these statistics with suspicion, not because they may be exaggerated, but because they may be too low. Not all assaults, robberies, and rapes are reported. And the statistics are constantly changing—not downward, but up. Recent reports show a drastic rise in burglary related crimes—crimes such as assault, rape, child molesting, and murder. And these aren't the only statistics.

· Every 33 seconds another automobile is stolen.

· In one year (1972) over 1 million cars were stolen.

How can you protect yourself when you are away from your home or office? Unless you are licensed to carry a gun, and know how to use one, carrying a gun offers no protection. If you are faced with a knife or gun, surrender your valuables as quietly and as quickly as possible. Being robbed is insulting, degrading, and demeaning, to say nothing of the fact that you may have worked hard for your money, and that the financial loss may cause you worry and deprivation. No matter. Loss of life or a serious injury is worse.

If you must walk alone and you do want protection, you can get some measure of it from a dog. Not any dog, by any means, but one that is trained to respond to your command. The ordinary household pet can be dragooned into watchdog services, but classifying all dogs as the same is about as sensible as classifying all people as the same. Your dog may very well be more afraid of strangers than you are. If you do get a trained dog, make sure you follow the trainer's suggestions to the letter. A dog can be spoiled, just as a child or an adult can be spoiled.

A chemical spray such as Mace or a police whistle may be helpful, depending entirely on you and also on the circumstances in which you find yourself. You can be sure the person trying to rob you isn't going to stand around and wait while you rummage around in your pocketbook for your chemical spray. A whistle is somewhat better, but by the time you recover from your shock you'll probably find that your assailant has long since gone. The best method, then, is anticipation. Try to avoid situations that will make you a victim. Stay in lighted places, walk or travel when others do. If your apartment has a laundry room, make arrangements with a neighbor (several would be better) to use this facility jointly. You are a likely victim if you enter your elevator alone with your arms loaded with packages. And don't invite strangers to your apartment. Your intentions may be good, but you may be the only one having such intentions.

However, if you ever feel a gun shoved into your back, or

find yourself facing one, don't try to be a hero. You may go the rest of your life and never be held up at gunpoint. Or, it could happen tomorrow. Armed robbery and assault with a deadly weapon—like auto theft, burglary, and extortion—are increasing every year, although there is now some evidence that the rate of crime growth is beginning to level off. There are no hard and fast rules to go by should you suddenly be looking down the barrel of a gun or feel the thrust of cold steel against your back. Most authorities agree, however, that if this does happen to you, it is wisdom to yield to the demands of the gunman rather than to attempt to counteract with some sudden movement of your own.

Since most armed robbers are after money or other valuables, it is sensible to do exactly as you are told, quietly and carefully. This may be difficult under traumatic circumstances such as these, but you can gain some degree of comfort, should it happen to you, in the knowledge that your assailant is in all probability as frightened as you are, and wants to leave you and the scene of the crime as rapidly as possible.

But isn't there anything you can do, without risk to yourself?

Yes, there is, and that is to keep your wits and use your powers of observation to the fullest extent. Note the height, weight, age, and coloring of the criminal. Look for distinguishing features or characteristics. Try to remember color of hair, color of eyes, marks on the face—anything that will help the police. Try to remember the sound of the voice. Observe the kind of clothing your assailant is wearing, or anything at all that is unusual about him. If a car is used, make a mental note of the license number, or if not, at least something about the car that would be helpful in identifying it. And then report your mishap to the police as quickly as possible.

It is easy to give advice, and much more difficult to be the victim of a crime. Being a crime victim and emotional shock go hand in hand, but, if you want to fight back, then this is possibly the best way you can do it.

While you may not be able to prevent a robbery, you may be able to minimize the possibility by taking evasive action or by reducing the consequences. If, for example, you must deposit a large sum of money in the bank every day, increase the number of trips you take, and reduce the amount you carry. Don't ever carry more cash with you than you really need. And some people are so credit-card happy that they may carry a dozen or more of them at all times. A credit card is more than cash, for it is an unlimited demand on your resources. Restrict your credit cards to those that are absolutely essential. Possession of a large number of credit cards is regarded as a status symbol by some, but it is a symbol that carries high personal risk.

Chapter 2

How to Make
Your Home More Secure

Your home is where you live. It can be nothing more than a single-room apartment, or a private house with a dozen rooms. Your motel room or your hotel room is your home for as long as you occupy it. If you rent a beach cabana, it is your home for the short period of time you use it. A home, then, isn't always a place you own, nor is it necessary for you to stay in it for years, months, or days. If you live, eat, and sleep in a trailer, then that is your home. But no matter what sort of residence you occupy, sooner or later—and often sooner—someone may get the idea that you represent a prospective victim. There is a stereotyped conception of the burglar as a rough, uneducated individual, usually preferring force, and dressed like a bum. Untrue. Burglars are people and like all people can be so well-dressed that you could not possibly imagine their profession. Some are extremely well-educated, highly cultured, amusing, witty, pleasant, courteous, and kindly. They are also crooks.

Burglary is a crime against a place or against property, not against people; or, more appropriately, only against people indirectly. In other words, it is technically a structure that is victimized, although in common usage we refer to the residents or owners of the structures as victims.

There is a difference between a burglar and the bunco operator described later, in Chapter 4. A burglar looks for likely places to rob while a con man looks for likely people to swindle. They both have the same objective. It is only their approach that is different.

Burglars often become aware of the ease with which entry can be made from clues left through the carelessness of victims. Doors and windows are often left unlocked, or in many cases even when they are locked, the locks are worthless and easily forced by the burglar with a celluloid strip or other simple tool. The burglar is often notified of the victim's absence from the premises through clues ranging from the obvious three-day accumulation of newspapers to the more subtle lone living-room light shining away brightly at three o'clock in the morning. The local obituary columns and society pages can notify the burglar of places ripe for theft, as may comments made by potential victims or persons associated with these potential victims—servants, beauticians, or bartenders, for example—regarding a given person's wealth and the occasions of his absence.

The burglar keeps up with the times and as a result steals more television sets than horses. Similarly, checks and credit cards have become more important targets of burglars in recent years.

The number and types of skills demonstrated by burglars are varied. They range from the relatively simple technique of throwing a rock through a window to gain entry, to the more complex use of lock-picking tools to overcome the barriers erected by the cautious property owner.

Similarly, a burglar's degree of skill is often shown in the types of goods he steals. The relatively unskilled or amateur burglar will generally seek money as his object of theft since this loot requires no knowledge of fences for disposal. On the other hand, the professional burglar has a wider number of contacts with receivers of stolen goods and the ability to distinguish between valuable and worthless items, a necessary ability in the case of furs or jewelry, for example. He will often make this type of goods his prime target.

The highly skilled burglar is less common than the unskilled or semiskilled type, and the majority of burglaries that do occur are a result of opportunity: A thief sees promising circumstances—a window that looks partially open, a doorstep with an accumulation of newspapers, mail, and milk bottles—and takes advantage of them at that time. Some burglars develop what could be called the "larceny sense," the ability to sensitize themselves to a variety of illicit opportunities.

Burglary is basically a passive crime and one in which the burglar tries to avoid any form of contact with the victim. The reasons for this are varied. First, the chances of getting caught after committing a crime in an unoccupied house are lower because of the high probability that the burglar will be gone from the scene of the crime, and possibly rid of the stolen goods, before the burglary is discovered. Second, entering unoccupied premises has the advantage of minimizing the risk of later identification. Third, even if the burglar is caught, the penalties for this type of crime are likely to be less severe than those for other forms of theft, such as robbery. Fourth, the burglar is usually fearful of encountering his victim, realizing that such a meeting may endanger his own life as well as increase the risk of his apprehension or severe punishment.

Within the general category of burglary, there are a variety of choices that the burglar can make. Some decide to be daytime burglars, working only during the day on vacant homes. Others prefer to steal at night; among them the so-called cat burglars, who like to enter while the victim is in, although characteristically do not generally seek a direct confrontation with him. Still other kinds include the hotel burglar, the jet-set burglar, and the apartment burglar.

The more highly skilled burglar may temporarily be dissuaded from committing a crime because of the unexpected occurrence of unforseen obstacles. A burglar will usually go ahead with a burglary once he has decided to do it, unless he encounters one particular indicator: noise. Any kind of noise creates uncertainty and noise is the burglar's main concern and fear. In most instances, however, once the burglar has made a successful entry he will usually complete a burglary, unless he discovers someone on the premises. Another factor that strongly affects the outcome of burglary attempts and the general level of burglary is police activity.

There are a variety of routes through which the burglar disposes of his stolen goods. They range from the "square john" man on the street—who purchases, say, a color-television receiver at an abnormally low price, perhaps suspecting that the item has been stolen but reluctant to ask any questions—to the professional fence who "contracts for" large quantities of stolen goods to supplement his legitimate business or, in some cases, to operate a business entirely based on the sale of stolen goods.

For many burglars, a trustworthy fence is the key to a successful burglary. The fence provides the burglar with an outlet for stolen goods that, for various reasons, he may not care to dispose of through pawnshops or on the street. Furthermore, by being able to sell stolen goods immediately, the professional thief avoids the pitfalls of the novice who is very often caught with the items in his possession because he lacks a place to merchandise them quickly.

The exact relationship between the fence and the burglar is variable. The drug addict, desperate for a fix, may sell his goods at an extraordinarily low price, whereas the more highly skilled burglar, well-trained in the art of burglary, will often use more than one fence as an outlet for his goods, both to increase his bargaining position and to avoid the danger of the loss of an entire haul in the event that any single fence is caught.

There is a difference between burglary and robbery. A place cannot be robbed, but a person can be. Robbery is stealing from a person either through the use of force or intimidation.

Taking property belonging to someone else is larceny. The laws that define robbery, burglary, and larceny vary from state to state, and in some burglary is predicated on unlawful entry.

A professional burglar with a successful record of three hundred break-ins told a Seattle newspaper that, based on his experience, "A good house burglar works only from just before dark until ten thirty or eleven P.M. when people might come home." He masks himself in many types of garb. He may wear a dinner jacket one time, and wear work clothes another. On other occasions he may carry a vacuum cleaner or a briefcase. "You have to look natural and appear to fit in," he said. "If you act like you own the place, nobody pays any attention."

When planning a job, he sometimes phones to find out if anyone is at home. If nobody answers the doorbell, he takes out a finely honed screwdriver, slips it between the lock and door jam, and gives it a flip. The door almost always opens.

A good burglar must know his lights. A bathroom light on, according to this burglar, is hardest to figure. "You can't tell if anyone is home, especially if the bathroom door is left open so the light shines out. And timers that turn lights on and off gives me fits."

The celluloid strip and the sharpened screwdriver aren't the only tools of the burglar. Some burglars prefer not carrying more tools than these since, if caught, there is little evidence that they planned to break and enter. But some burglars will not consider a job without a good assortment of not only various sizes and shapes of screwdrivers, but glass cutters, wire coat hangers (easily shaped as the job requires), gear pullers, lock pullers, a hacksaw, a crowbar (especially helpful where considerable force may be needed), lock pickers, auto jacks, etc. And some burglars carry no tools at all. They may simply move from house to house or from apartment door to apartment door, trying for one that has accidentally been left open. When they find one, they ring the doorbell and have some sort of ready question to ask if someone does come to the door. If no one answers after repeated rings, then they are in and out in a flash, grabbing and taking anything that seems to have value. They are familiar with the most favored hiding places and are quite adept at locating your cache of cash and jewelry in a hurry.

It would be a mistake to think that everything is in favor of the burglar, although the home owner or apartment dweller is often most cooperative. Time is one of the burglar's greatest enemies. Even though he is ransacking a place that quite obviously has no occupants, he does not know when they will return, or when he may be observed by a neighbor. Some burglars allow themselves not more than a few minutes for each job. If, within the time limit they have set for themselves, they are unable to find anything of value or that they regard of value, they leave. No burglar will remain on a job indefinitely, unless he has some knowledge that the occupants will definitely not return for a long time.

What should you do if you surprise a burglar at work in your home or apartment? The first thing to do is not to panic. Most burglars do not carry guns, but in a tight situation they can make use of some heavy tools they may have in their possession as weapons. It may not be easy to remember as many physical characteristics as possible, but try to do so. Make a mental record of height, weight, possible nationality, complexion, color of eyes. Were the eyes normal, alert, or droopy? Any visible scars, marks, or tattoos? Approximate age? Wearing a hat? Color of hair and way it is cut? Beard, mustache, sideburns? Shirt, necktie, jacket, or coat? Weapon, if any? Right- or left-handed? Kind and color of trousers? Shoes?

Yes, it would take an extraordinary individual to note and remember all of these items, and you may consider yourself cool, calm, and collected if you manage to recall half of them. But, we repeat, don't be a hero, and unless you are regularly accustomed to strenuous physical effort, don't try it at this moment. Don't use it as an opportunity to prove your manhood. If you have the burglar cornered, he will fight that way, knowing that he could lose his life or spend many years in prison. All you are fighting for is property, and that's replaceable. And if you feel like screaming, don't. You will give the burglar no alternative but to silence you. And, as soon as it is safe to do so, call the police. If you don't remember the number to call, just dial the operator.

How Not to Cooperate with the Burglar

1. When you are planning a trip, don't "tell" the burglar you are on vacation. Maybe you remembered to notify the milk-man, but what about the newspapers? Call your newspaper office and tell them you do not want delivery of the paper. Don't schedule it for the exact day you are to leave, but start-ing several days earlier. The reason for this is to make sure the newspaper will follow your instructions. It is entirely possible for someone to take your message and to forget it or ignore it. Also, have the renewal date of delivery set for three or four days after your return, but not on the day you come back. Again, this is designed to give you a margin of safety in the event you cannot return on the day you expect.

You cannot stop delivery of mail, but you can make arrangements with a cooperative neighbor to pick up your mail every day, and also to remove any newspapers, circulars, packages, and deliveries left at your doorstep. The newspaper may not be your regular paper, but may be instead a "free sample" or one that was left at your door in error. Don't just pick any neighbor, but one you can trust and preferably one who is obligated to you in some way, someone for whom you have done a number of favors.

2. You are often advised to turn on a light and to leave it turned on while you are away. That's nonsense. Yes, do turn on a light, but remember that a strong light burning in your living room at three o'clock in the morning is a dead giveaway that you aren't home. Instead, buy several timers. These are in-expensive, simple devices that will turn lights on and off for you. Use one for a transistor radio set so that it will turn the set on during the hours that people habitually listen. Don't set it for the wee hours of the morning! The station may not be on, and if it is, the sound (in the quiet of the night), will not only annoy your neighbors but will alert burglars that your home is ready for picking.

If you do use timers—and you should—put one lamp in the

bathroom with the door kept open. Put the other in the kitchen. And use the third in the bedroom. Do not set the timers so that they all go on and off at the same time. Arrange them so that as one turns on, the others turn off.

3. Have an automatic record player turn on, with a record playing of a dog barking.

4. Do not pull down all your shades. If you have window shades, keep them in their normal position. How many people live in homes in which the shades are pulled all the way down for twenty-four hours? The whole idea is to give your home a "lived-in" look that will discourage burglars. And this applies to venetian blinds, also.

5. If you have a lawn, shrubbery, and outside flowers, make arrangements with someone to mow the lawn, trim the shrubbery, and make sure the flowers are tended.

6. Be sure to close and lock all windows and doors, including the garage door. This sounds so basic you may wonder why it is included, but in the last-minute excitement of packing and departure, a window or screen may be overlooked. It pays to take the time to double-lock doors and double check everything.

7. Make a "security" check list just to make certain you do not forget anything. Prepare this check list several days before you leave and do some thinking about it between the time you first prepare it and the time you say goodbye. Then, just before you leave check off each item on the list to make sure you have followed your own instructions. Take the list along with you on your trip. There is nothing more guaranteed to ruin a vacation than to wonder whether you closed and locked the kitchen window, or whether you remembered to set the lighting timers.

8. Be sure to leave your house key with a neighbor. This can be a reciprocal agreement. Ask your neighbor to check your house occasionally to see if everything is alright. If possible, give your neighbor an emergency phone number where you can be reached. If your neighbor agrees to your "check my house" request, ask that the check be done in the evening as well as in the daytime. Most home burglaries take place in the daytime, but the nighttime act of turning lights on and off

tends to keep burglars away. Also, ask your neighbor *not* to make the checks at the same time each day but to vary them. The checks should not be routine, but haphazard.

9. Notify your local police department. Tell them when you are leaving and when you plan to return. Let them know whom you have authorized to enter your home while you are gone. The police will make every effort to cooperate with you by keeping your home under periodic surveillance. If you must do this by telephoning your local police station, do so, but it is better to make a personal visit. This will not only make your request more emphatic, but will give the police an opportunity to learn who you are. Instead of just being a voice, you will be a person.

10. Don't tell strangers anything. If you are sociable, like people and mingle with others, do so; but do not confide your "going-away" plans to anyone. Actually, the fewer the number of people who know about your trip, the safer your home or apartment will be. There are some who must know—the police, your neighbor, and your employer, if you have one. And do not discuss your vacation plans on the phone. You can be overheard and you never know who is listening in.

Your local newspaper may have a social column, listing the activities of people in your community. Do *not* contact them just to get your name in the paper. There will be enough time for that when you return.

11. Be careful to whom you send picture postcards while you are away. The best method is to time the mailing of the postcards so they are delivered just as you return home.

12. Don't keep extra valuables at home. Do not keep spare cash at home. Deposit your spare cash in your bank and put your valuables in a safety deposit box in your local bank. Do not put cash in your safety box.

13. Write the serial numbers of expensive equipment you must leave at home. This includes your television set (or sets), typewriters, hi-fi equipment, and expensive tools. Use an engraving tool to mark all your equipment with your name. This may not add to the appearance of the equipment, but it will make it much more difficult for the burglar to "fence," plus

the fact that the fence may either not accept such marked equipment, or may offer a substantially lower price. Keep your equipment record in a safe place, preferably your bank vault.

14. If you have a dog, don't take him with you. He is excellent home and apartment protection, if he is the right kind of dog and has been selected with security in mind. But you must make sure he is watered, fed, and exercised every day.

15. If you have a private home, equip it with outside weather-resistant floodlamps. Connect these to automatic timers inside the house, and arrange to have them come on when the automatically controlled lights in the house go off.

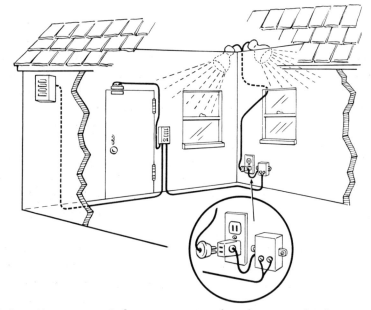

Automatic-power-switch arrangement for the control of external floodlights. When the door is opened, the external alarm sounds and the area outside the house is flooded with light. (Hydrometals, Inc.)

16. Don't ever leave a key under the doormat or any other hiding place. If, for practical reasons, you must do so, at least select a place that will be difficult for the burglar to find. For apartment dwellers this is practically impossible, plus the fact that sooner or later someone will see you doing it. Most burglaries—the greatest percentage by far—are by direct entry by the burglar right through the front door.

17. Always keep in mind that burglary is quite often a crime of opportunity and whether it is successful or not depends on how vulnerable you are.

18. Never, under any circumstances, leave your credit card (or cards) at home.

19. Burglars respect properly installed safes and locks, provided these are the right types. A burglar can look at a lock and learn from it just how security-conscious you are. There is probably no lock a determined burglar cannot open, but burglars must work against time. If they abandon an attempt at entry, it isn't because they cannot overcome the lock; simply that it would take much too much time to do so.

20. If you move into a new home or a new apartment, either have the lock tumblers reset, or, better yet, install new locks.

21. Make sure you have a chain lock on the front door. The usual type of spring-latch lock (this is the type that snaps shut when you close the door) is also a "snap" for the burglar. A burglar can open a spring-latch lock just about as fast as you can.

22. Most people have a habit of combining their house keys and car keys on the same key ring or in the same key holder. There is nothing wrong with this, but if you must leave your car key with a parking-lot attendant, leave only the car key. It is very easy for anyone with a mind for doing so to duplicate your house key. And he can get your home address from your license-plate number.

23. If you use an electronic telephone-answering device, always put a message on the tape that you expect to return momentarily, even if you expect to be away for several days. Never supply strangers with personal information. A common trick is to use the "survey" approach. "We are making a survey

for [and here the caller will mention a well-known company] and would like to know. . . ." Do not supply financial information, data about your possessions (number of cars, TV sets, cameas, typewriters), etc.

24. Do not admit strangers to your home. They may seem respectable, pleasant, charming, well-dressed. But so are a lot of burglars. They may be giving your home a "pre-examination" to determine if it is worth burglarizing.

25. Does your front door have an attractive large glass panel? Does your door also have equally attractive side glass panels? A burglar with a brick enclosed in a heavy rag can make short work of it and do it fairly quietly, or else get through with glass cutters. Once the glass is removed, a burglar can reach in and open the door lock. Use a metal grillwork to cover the glass.

26. If any street lights on which you depend are broken or inoperative, report them to your town or city authorities at once. Burglars dislike lights. Why improve their working conditions?

27. Be aware and beware of strangers, particularly if you see them loitering near your home or the home of a neighbor. If you are at all suspicious, telephone your neighbor so that you can both keep an eye on the activities. Burglars often "case" or examine homes they regard as likely prospects for their activities. Further, the burglar may be very well-dressed, appear conservative, and drive a well-kept, expensive-looking car. He may look more like a very successful business-man or a business executive than a burglar.

28. Keep your patio doors locked, preferably from the inside. A strip of wood on the inside bottom track will help prevent the door from being opened from the outside.

29. When you leave your house, close your garage doors. Open garage doors and an empty garage are a positive indication of an empty house. And don't just close the garage doors—lock them.

30. If you've been painting or repairing around your home, put all ladders away when you are finished with them. Put them inside and store them so that they aren't easily removed.

As an alternative to the nuisance of carrying ladders in and out of the house, lock them with a steel chain and a sturdy lock to some sort of strong fastener. This will also help keep your ladders from "walking away."

31. If you must do some work in your basement, or in your attic, or in your garage, or in any area that is away from the house proper, consider your house as unoccupied and act accordingly. Lock your front door, and any other doors, and keep your windows locked. If you have a dog that can act and behave as a watchdog, don't have him keep you company. Let him stay on guard duty where he belongs.

32. Do not leave any valuable articles outside your home. This includes bicycles, lawnmowers, tools, and children's toys. Burglary can take place right outside your home, as well as inside. If you do not plan to use your car, keep it inside the garage. If you do intend using it, keep the car doors locked and the car windows closed, and the side vent windows closed and locked. Cars can be and are being stolen from the driveway. Even if you leave your car just for a few minutes to go into your house, act toward your car as though you were going to leave it for hours.

33. Get into the habit of making a security check at night before you go to bed. Are all windows secured and locked? Is the front door locked? Are all windows and doors on your sun deck and porch locked? If you have a basement, are all possible places of entry locked?

34. Try not to get into a "I'm leaving the house" routine. If possible, try to leave at different times and try to return at different times. Try to give your house the appearance of being lived in constantly. The greater the traffic flow in and out of your home or apartment, the less the chances for a burglary. If your family has a number of members, try not to leave together and try not to return together. An exodus, en masse, from your home can inspire only one interpretation.

35. If you live in an apartment and the mail is delivered after you leave for work in the morning (as it probably is) try to arrange with a neighbor to remove your mail as early in the day as possible. All a burglar has to do is check the com-

munity mailbox in an apartment house to learn which apartments may be vacant and which may be occupied. If you are a single woman, never put your full name on the mailbox. Use your first initial and be sure to omit Mrs., Miss, or Ms. Physically, an unarmed burglar will feel he is more than a match for any female. There is nothing wrong with the fem lib spirit, and women are fully entitled to all male privileges and prerogatives. But identifying yourself is a poor tradeoff for which you get nothing in return, except possible trouble.

36. If you live in an apartment house, form a mutual-protection society with the neighbors on your floor. In many apartments the occupants tend to be withdrawn and unsociable, but for your mutual protection you should form some sort of patrol system so that corridors are watched. You will also find it helpful to post a sign in the corridor that it is being watched and that all the neighbors on that floor are highly security-conscious. Report any strangers on your floor to the superintendent at once. Organize the "buddy" system mentioned earlier when you go shopping or use the inside laundry in your apartment house. And remember, never enter an elevator with an arm full of packages together with a stranger. Try to arrange to do your shopping and your laundry with a neighbor, and preferably with a group.

37. If you must leave your home or your apartment when you go out in the evening, leave a light burning and a radio playing quietly. Always try to give the impression that someone is home. If you have a dog, he should be trained to bark when the front doorbell rings, if he does not do so instinctively.

38. Two locks are always better than one. Put supplementary locks on any window or door that gets constant usage. Be especially sure to lock any windows that open onto or are near fire escapes. In apartment houses, toilet windows near fire escapes are quite often left unlocked and are often used as a means of entry by a burglar. Even if the window is several floors above ground, lock it. If you have doors or windows facing an outside balcony, and that balcony is several stories above ground, lock them. A competent burglar doesn't always use an elevator or stairway, but can move from one floor to

another by climbing up outside balconies.

39. If you must have maid service in your home or apartment, be sure to check references and do so thoroughly and carefully. Never put temptation in anyone's way. Keep your liquor locked up, and do not keep cash and/or jewelry in an easily opened drawer. The advantage to having a maid working in your home is that it is occupied during her working time. The disadvantage is that the maid is a stranger. It is better to hire someone recommended by a friend or neighbor and who has worked for them for a number of years. Even if the hourly rate is higher, it is safer. If possible, do not have the maid report on a regular schedule, but try to stagger her working hours from week to week.

Despite all your precautions and in the face of every effort you may have made, it is still possible for your home or apartment to be burglarized. If a burglar is sufficiently determined, if he has enough time, if he can work in the dark, and if he is reasonably sure of not being interrupted, you can be the victim of a successful burglary.

Then why bother with these anti-burglary measures? The more you do, the more security-conscious you become and the greater the odds in your favor. They can never be 100 percent, but you can make robbing your home or apartment so difficult, so time-consuming, and so nerve-racking for the burglar, that he will pass you by to try another place. Burglars, like the rest of us, are human beings, and do not like to work any harder than necessary, nor do they like to take any more chances than required.

What to Do if You Have Been "Burgled"

If you return home, only to find that you have been robbed, there are a few things you should do, and some you should not do.

1. Do not panic. Try to remain calm.

2. Leave the apartment and use the nearest telephone to call the police. The burglar may still be in your apartment when you return, and if he hears you telephoning the police, may

try to restrain you—forcibly.

3. Do not touch anything in your apartment. Even if the house or apartment looks like a mess—drawers opened and contents dumped on the floor, sofa ripped apart, etc.—don't touch it. You may destroy valuable evidence or fingerprints the police may need to help catch the burglar. Police work is difficult, tedious, and time-consuming. Work with your police; not against them.

4. Don't try suddenly to become a detective or personal investigator, unless, of course, you are a professional, in which case this advice isn't necessary. A trained detective will be able to read much more from the burglary than you possibly can.

5. Cooperate with your police department. It does not help to harangue any police investigator with complaints of inadequate police protection. Instead, give them any information you have, and as much information as you can supply. This includes a description of what was taken, serial numbers of stolen equipment, amount of money and/or jewelry stolen, etc. If you've noticed any strangers in the area, furnish the police with a description, including a description of any automobile that aroused your suspicions.

6. Take color photos of your most prized possessions—jewelry, furs, rugs, paintings—and keep these photos together with your inventory list in your bank vault. If you are burglarized, give the police these photos in addition to your descriptions. Do not destroy the negatives of these pictures. It may be necessary for you to give the police duplicate pictures, and you should keep an extra set for yourself. Keep copies of the prints, together with your inventory list and serial numbers in your safety-deposit box. If you are insured against burglary, your insurance agent may suggest that you let him hold a duplicate set. This will help you when you file your insurance claim.

Finally, there is something you can do to stop the growing burglary rate—and it is growing. You can stop saying, "Why don't the police do something?" Instead, become security-conscious.

Take every possible security measure you can in your home

or apartment. The more difficult you make it for burglars, the more likely it is that they will go into some other line of work.

Don't be a loner. Become interested in your neighborhood and work together with your neighbors for your mutual aid and protection. Speak to your local police about setting up your own self-protection group. They are experienced and should give you the benefit of their accumulated knowledge.

Finally, cooperate with the police and any other law-enforcement agencies. Become involved. Just because a burglary happens next door to you is no reason to give a sigh of relief. Instead, look on it as a warning. A burglar likes to pick off his victims one at a time. Why let him have his own way?

What Should You Do in an Emergency?

The best thing to do about an emergency is to try to avoid it. Upon returning to your house or apartment, be alert to the possibility that someone may have forced entry while you were gone. Don't just rush into your home. Take a quick glance at your windows and your door to see if you can observe anything unusual or different. Some burglars leave doors and windows open, not as their calling cards, but as a means of quick exit should it become necessary. If you do see some evidence of entry, stay out; and, immediately, get to a telephone and call the police. They are equipped with experience, and, if necessary, have weapons and know how to use them. Further, you won't have to explain anything to the police should you (which is unlikely) succeed in capturing and overcoming the burglar.

If you are a light sleeper, if you are disturbed by the slightest noise, or if you fall asleep aware of the possibility that you may be burglarized, you can be sure of one thing. You aren't going to get a good night's sleep since all the conditions are against it.

Under these circumstances, the best thing to do is to install a lock on your door. Don't use a key-type lock, since, in case of fire, you may want to get out of the room in a hurry. Instead, install a barrel bolt. These are slide bolts, usually cylindrical, and can be screwed to the door and door jamb by wood screws. They come in various sizes but the smaller ones, usually about two inches, can be ripped off the door with one strong push. Get a sturdy one that is about five inches long. And use it. It isn't intended as a decoration. Barrel bolts are designed with cutouts holding the handle of the bolt in position, so these bolts cannot be pushed back by an intruder on the other side of the door.

Barrel bolts are intended for use with all-wooden doors. If your bedroom door has glass panes, it would be relatively easy for a burglar to remove the pane, slip his hand inside, and slide the bolt back. For a glass door, then, you will need some type of keyed lock. Be sure to mount the key somewhere near the door, but well out of the reach of a probing arm. Remember where the key is if you should need to leave the room in a hurry.

As an alternative to the barrel bolt, you can use a swinging hook and screw eye. The swinging hook is fastened to the door; the screw eye to the door frame. This is easier to mount than a barrel bolt, and costs less, but doesn't provide as much protection. A burglar can slip a thin knife or shim between the edge of the door and the jamb and lift the swinging hook out of position. But if this is what you prefer, get one that is fairly substantial. The small ones pull out much too easily.

If you do have a bedroom lock of some kind, get into the habit of making sure that the bedroom door is locked before you retire. There is no point in having a lock unless you use it. And if you have a lock, be sure to have a telephone in the bedroom. This will enable you to phone for help. Otherwise, you will be a prisoner in your own bedroom while the burglar ransacks the rest of the house.

You can also get a very economical, battery-operated door alarm for your bedroom door. Such door alarms are completely self-contained. They contain a buzzer, a battery, and a switch that is closed when the bedroom door is opened. The entire unit is small and can be mounted directly on the door. The door-operated alarm—actually just a buzzer—is no substitute for a true alarm system. The sound it produces will be enough to awaken you, but it may not be loud enough to deter a burglar. It all depends on the burglar, his determination to rob you, and the kind of valuables he expects to find. It also depends on the kind of person you are. Many people prefer sleeping through a burglary, and would rather not have the shock of an encounter.

Even with a telephone and a barrel bolt on the door you still have a problem. Although you phone the police immediately, there is no assurance they will arrive before the persistent burglar gets through the door. A professional burglar, hearing you telephone the police, will make for the nearest exit—and quickly. He is smart enough to know that his risk factor has suddenly gone up considerably. Your thief, though, may be an amateur. He may be high on drugs or alcohol. He may be a mental case. He may think you are alone, weak, helpless, frightened. Or, he may not think at all, but will be in a fit of unreasoning rage. He may be strong enough to push through the door, not caring how much noise he makes, or that the police may very well be on their way.

As protection, you should have something with which you can defend yourself. Keep a golf club handy. Or, a broom handle. Or, a length of round metal rod of the kind used for drapes. Or, a baseball bat. Whichever one of these you select, do two things: (1) Keep it somewhere near your bed; and (2) get accustomed to handling it. Do not keep a loaded gun in or near your night table unless you have a permit for the gun, unless you know how to use one, and unless a gun is part of your usual business activities.

Viewer vs. Chain

The advantage of a chain guard is that it lets you open your front door a few inches, permitting you to see who is calling and to receive moderately sized packages, while restricting entry to someone on the other side of your door.

There are two basic types of chain guards—those with a keyed lock, and those that do not have a keyed lock. If you have a chain guard that isn't the locking type, a dextrous burglar can put his foot against your partially opened door, and then reach in and unchain the lock. He can't do this if the chain is a locking type.

However, whether the chain is a locking type or not, if the burglar is husky enough, he can throw his weight against the door and pull the chain right off its screwmount.

And so, as an alternative, it is better to have a viewer mounted on your door. The viewer lets you see who is at your door, without opening it. If you have the slightest suspicion of your caller, keep your door closed.

The best arrangement is a combination of viewer and locked door chain. When someone comes to your door and rings the bell, it is almost an instinctive reaction to swing the door open. Don't. Instead look through your viewer, and if you are satisfied that the message or package for you is legitimate, then unlock your slide chain fastener.

Viewers are more generally used on apartment house doors since that is the only way you can see who is outside the door. With a house, the visitor can be seen through any front window. If your apartment door doesn't have a viewer, discuss your need for a viewer with the landlord or building-management personnel. The usual arrangement is that you will be permitted to do so if you will bear the expense, if you will pay for any possible damage to the door, and if you will agree to have the viewer remain as the property of the landlord when you move. Once you overcome all these barriers, get a viewer having a wide angle of view. Some viewers are very restricted and aren't very helpful.

Chapter 3

Locks and
Alarm Systems

The purpose of a lock is simple. Its basic function is to keep the burglar out, and, insofar as it is capable of doing this, it will give you a sense of security. That's a psychological bonus, but whether you really earn it or not depends entirely on the kind of locks you use and whether you give them a chance to do their job—that is, if you keep them locked when they should be. A lock, the proper lock, is your first line of defense against burglars.

There is no lock a determined burglar cannot open. But to most burglars there are three essential requirements to the success of his act: time, quiet, and darkness. It is not that a burglar cannot pick a particular lock you may have selected, simply that he cannot afford or is unwilling to trade his time against the possible risk of detection. And there is no such thing as a pick-proof lock. If you see one advertised as such, then the manufacturer is either deceiving himself, deceiving you, or both. A reputable manufacturer will advertise his locks as pick-resistant. But that leaves the manufacturer with an escape as wide as a barn door: How pick-resistant is pick-resistant?

There are basically two types of locks: active and passive. Very few active locks are made and only on order for highly valuable, highly specialized commercial protection. An active lock is one that fights back. It may contain a gun that will fire at any individual not authorized to open it. It may fire a gas, or spray a chemical mist. Some oldtime locks even had spring-loaded steel blades, ready to fly out at any intruder. The modern active lock (for the most part, but with a few exceptions) sets off an alarm or sends a signal to some externally located security office. Some locks are now being offered for home use that turn on the lights in all or a part of the house if tampered with; or that ring a bell, buzzer, or some other kind of alarm; or that may even connect with a security office or the police department.

Undoubtedly, the worst type of lock and one that offers just about no protection at all, is the spring-latch lock. This is an inexpensive lock and can easily be opened with a shim, also known as a cheater or a shove knife. All that the burglar requires is a small bit of heavy metal to use as a jimmy. Its purpose is to widen the distance between the door and its frame slightly, just enough to let the shim move in. The shim can be made out of anything that is flexible, but somewhat stiff. It can be a plastic ruler, one card out of a plastic deck of cards, part of a metal venetian blind, or a small bit of scrap celluloid. The burglar pushes the shim against the bolt of the spring lock, and because there is nothing to restrain its movement, the bolt moves back and the door opens.

You can recognize a spring-latch lock by its bolt, which has a beveled face and can be easily moved back and forth with your finger. This doesn't mean such locks cannot or should not be used. They are economical locks for keeping the door locked against the wind.

The spring latch, shown here, has a V-shaped bolt. It is adequate for inside doors connecting one room to another, but offers no security on an entrance door. (Schlage Lock Co.)

The bolt of a lock is the moving portion, which the strike is the part that receives the bolt and is fitted on the door jamb.

Still another rather easily opened lock is the type that is used on the front door of an apartment house and is opened by keys supplied to all the tenants. Since so many keys are distributed it is no great problem for a burglar to get one, but even this isn't really necessary. Such locks are also inexpensive types, are manufactured to rather loose tolerances, and can be "jiggled." Jiggling is the act of inserting a key or slim bit of metal into the keyway of the lock, and jiggling the metal until it raises the tumblers. The great problem with this kind of lock, as well as with the spring latch, is that it inspires a false sense of security. With these locks, there is no security.

There are a number of ways of preventing a burglar from using a shim. They all work the same way in the sense that they prevent the shim from being pushed into position, or resist the use of a jimmy bar. However, if you do have a spring-latch type, you can add a separate deadbolt lock. As an auxiliary lock, in combination with another keyed lock, a deadbolt will provide two-lock security. It is available as a single-cylinder or double-cylinder unit. The double cylinder is recommended where complete control is wanted. It is especially helpful for securing a door with glass panels. An intruder may break the glass to reach the inside knob, but will be defeated by the deadbolt that requires a key to unlock the door from the inside as well as the outside. There is one problem with this lock, however: It can be a safety hazard if you should ever need to use the door as an emergency exit. Use this type of deadbolt only as an auxiliary lock when the house is to be unoccupied. Or else, keep a spare key close to the door, where you can see it, but out of the reach of anyone trying to get in from the outside.

For normal residential locking, a precision-built bored cylindrical lock, with a deadlocking latch, should be considered the minimum acceptable security. This unit consists of a latch with an adjoining small plunger that is held depressed —or deadlocks—when the door is locked, making it impossible to release or push back the latch with the insertion of a shim between the latch and strike. For security with safety, this type of entrance lock should also have the "panic-proof" feature for immediate exit, with the latch retracting and unlocking the door with a turn of the inside knob in either direction.

Some locks are combination deadlocks and latches, such as the unit shown here. This does offer more security than a latch-type lock but is not as good as a separate deadlock. (Schlage Lock Co.)

A keyless lock, with a spring latch, is acceptable with either the cylindrical or tubular type of mechanism when used for passageway, bedroom, and closet doors where security isn't required.

There are a tremendous variety of locks available, each with special features that make it jimmy- and pick-proof. One type consists of a combination of a half-inch throw (or projection) deadlocking latch and a one-inch-throw deadbolt in which is concealed a hardened steel roller that resists sawing or prying. The lock mechanism is protected by an armor plate under an ornamental rose, and the cylinder is recessed to discourage forceful entry. When the door is locked, the outside knob is free-spinning so that it is impossible to get leverage on it to force or twist it. It is also panic-proof since both bolt and latch retract simultaneously for immediate exit with a twist of the inside knob.

There are all sorts of auxiliary locks available, many of which are easy to install. In addition to the standard deadbolt, a vertical bolt lock offers reliable security. You can also install a rim lock above your existing lock.

Still another fine lock is the Segalock Jimmy Proof, designed to provide a lock that can be deadbolted and out of reach of a jimmy bar. This lock is a rim type with the lock housing on the door and the strike on the door frame. The bolt is vertical and drops through the holes in a one-piece solid bronze casting that acts as the strike.

Burglars have an answer to the jimmy-proof lock. They have a choice of such tools as grip vice pliers, pincers, or gear pullers to help pull the entire cylinder out. Once the cylinder of the lock is out, it is easy for the burglar to reach in and move the bolt out of the strike. But for every technique of the burglar there is a counter technique. In this case you can get an armor-plated front from your locksmith to put over the outside-lock housing. This prevents the grip vice pliers or pincers from getting a grip on the lock cylinder. Still another form of protection is an armor collar, a circular ring of tough metal that fits around the cylinder. It is free to turn and so when a burglar uses pincers, all that happens is that the collar turns, but the cylinder remains firmly in place.

Increase your security by using a door chain. And, remember, a burglar can use a bent coat hanger to move the usual type of door chain out of the way. With a lock-type door chain, however, after a burglar has managed to defeat the regular door lock, the door opens just a few inches and cannot be opened further unless the lock on the door chain can be defeated. A cheap door chain can be easily snipped; the better grades use hardened metal requiring a powerful tool for cutting. The lock-type door chain is excellent for use with doors that have glass panels. A burglar that removes a pane of glass only to find himself thwarted by the chain lock may have second thoughts about jimmying off the lock.

When you buy a lock, consider it the way you do insurance. You aren't buying a lock; you are buying protection. A quality lock, properly installed, should last the life of the house. If you select a bored lock—either tubular or cylindrical—for a new door or to replace a worn-out lock, you should be able to install it yourself if you have average mechanical ability and the tools normally found in a home shop. However, if you have special locking problems—for example, your front door may be metal instead of wood, or it may have an artistic design—it would be best to locate a firm that specializes in builder's hardware to advise you. Or, you may want to consult a locksmith who qualifies as a security expert or master locksmith. He will probably include security consultation and inspection in his services; he also can sell and install locks.

Specialty Locks

Not all locks require keys. One type, known as a Simplex, is a pushbutton combination type. Instead of a key, there are five pushbuttons on the outside, but to unlock you must not only know the correct buttons to push, but you must also know the correct sequence. Any combination can be set using as many of the five buttons as you wish in any sequence you want. The buttons can be pushed individually or together with one or more of the other buttons as part of the special combination. For example, a combination of 2 and 4 pushed together, then 3, then 5, is not the same as 2, 4, 3, and 5 pushed individually and in that sequence. The lock will open only when the correct buttons are pushed in the proper order. The Simplex locks have a heavy-duty cast construction, an all-brass face plate, and opaque nylon buttons. The force-proof front knob assembly is designed to make forced entry impossible. And you can change the lock combination if you ever suspect that someone has managed to learn it. The advantage of a lock of this kind is that you can never forget your key or lose it.

Who Are the Burglars?

Burglaries have increased 13 percent since 1968 and 117 percent since 1960. It is very difficult to give exact figures since not all burglaries are reported, and furthermore the definition of exactly what is a burglary can vary from state to state. But one thing is certain. The average age of the burglar is getting lower. Arrests of juveniles for serious crimes increased 72 percent from 1960 to 1970. Eight out of ten burglary arrests were of persons under twenty-five years of age.

Burglaries have increased 13 percent since 1968 and 117 percent since 1960. Arrests of juveniles for serious crimes increased 72 percent from 1960 to 1970. Eight out of ten burglary arrests were of persons under twenty-five years of age.

The attitude of many burglars is typified in the following excerpt from an actual interview of a young house burglar arrested in Salt Lake City, Utah, and now serving time in Utah State Prison:

Question: How many burglaries have you made in the last two years?

Answer: Close to one thousand.

Question: Did you just go for the rich home?

Answer: No, man, the poorest homes have TV sets and stuff you can move in a hurry.

Question: What about dogs?

Answer: They didn't really give me a problem. Dogs outside can be fed or put out. If a dog is in a house, he usually thinks you belong there.

Question: You'd go into a home with a dog inside?

Answer: Yes.

Question: Why do you think people are complacent about protection?

Answer: Most think they don't have anything worth stealing.

Question: Have you ever been in a home where you couldn't find anything worth stealing?

Answer: No. I've even taken a lamp table.

Question: What would you do if you got into a home and didn't find what you were expecting?

Answer: I'd bust up the joint, kick in the TV, and let off steam in some way.

Question: What if you walked into a room and an alarm sounded?

Answer: Man, I'd split.

Burglars in America are now making "house calls" at the rate of five thousand per day. Using 1960 as the base year, by 1970 residency nighttime burglaries of residences were up 129 percent. In that same period daytime burglaries increased 337 percent. Law-enforcement agencies were successful in solving less than one out of every five cases of burglary in 1969. This low clearance rate indicates the lack of a deterrent and slight risk in detection. And a 1969 report by J. Edgar Hoover states further, "Since 1960 there has been a substantial increase of 387 percent in daytime residential burglaries. The causes—social, human and material—that contributed to these trends are beyond the immediate control of law-enforcement agencies."

An unenviable record. We now average over 1,759 burglaries per 100,000 people in metropolitan areas.

Break-in Types

Burglary isn't the only driving motive for breaking and entering your home. A burglar-proof lock—that is, a lock that is as burglar-proof as you can get—will help hold out not just the professional (and also amateur) burglar, but other undesirable types as well. The vandal breaks into a home for "kicks." He resents anyone who has anything, including just a happy home. If discovered while breaking up a house, he can be extremely dangerous.

The drug addict who has a fifty-to-one-hundred-dollar a day habit to support has only two ways to earn that kind of money. He either steals or pushes drugs. Most of them steal because there is less risk. They burglarize many times while high and under these circumstances are very dangerous.

The sex pervert breaks into the home while someone is there for very obvious reasons.

Now, assume that despite your best efforts, a burglar has managed to enter your home. This doesn't mean you are defeated, for you can still do a number of things every burglar fears. One of these is the sound of an alarm. One technique is a highly sophisticated and reliable intrusion-detection system (made by Gard-Site). This device creates an invisible electronic field with a detection potential of up to twelve hundred square feet around a control unit antenna. This electronic field is capable of penetrating most materials used in the construction of walls, partitions, and floors. When the burglar disturbs this field—and he does so simply by stepping into it—the waves created within the electronic field flow back to the antenna, which sets off the alarm.

This system, which can be installed in minutes, can be completely out of sight. The system is programmed with a two-and-a-half-minute delay to allow you to leave once it is activated. A delay period is also provided for you to return and deactivate the system.

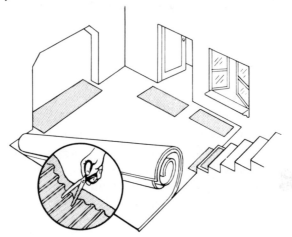

Mat switches are pressure-sensitive switches and can be positioned beneath scatter rugs, room-size rugs, floor, or step carpeting. Their advantage is that they are invisible. The problem is with the wiring connected to the switch. With wall-to-wall carpeting and with stair carpeting, all the wiring can be concealed. This is also the case if scatter rugs touch the wall. (Hydrometals, Inc.)

According to FBI statistics, only one in forty-one thousand intruders will remain when an alarm is sounded. They all fear detection. And there are any number of alarm intrusion devices you can use, from those that set off an alarm if a window is open or broken to those that sound with the opening of one, or more, doors in your home. Some use electronics, depending on a transmitted signal, while others are completely wired systems. One type uses an ordinary-looking mat that can be placed near the front door so that any intruder steps on it automatically. Or, it can be hidden under a rug and is activated when the burglar walks across it. The mat is a pressure-sensitive device, containing a switch wired to a battery-operated alarm.

The best deterrent for burglars is to have an occupied home, but even such a home is more secure with pick-resistant and jimmy-resistant locks installed by a professional locksmith. But if a home is not to be a prison, it must be a place you can leave with reasonable peace of mind and so it makes sense to have a sensitive intrusion alarm system. More popularly called burglar alarms, such systems offer continuous protection.

Regardless of their construction, design, application, or sophistication, all alarm systems have three functional elements: the sensor, control, and alarm. They may be separate devices or may be contained in a single housing, but all three elements must be present for effective operation.

The sensor, as its name implies, "senses" or detects a condition. Depending on its design, it may detect fire, smoke, a drop in temperature, humidity, sound, light, or movement. It can be as simple a device as an electrical switch or as complex as a TV camera.

The sensor works because of some movement by the burglar. The burglar, by the pressure of his feet, may close a switch. Or, he may break through a light beam. Or, he may disturb an electrical-field pattern set up in your home. Whatever the sensor may be, the burglar causes it to sense, or become aware of, some change in conditions. And when this happens, the sensor sends a signal to a control device. The control then sets off the alarm. In the simplest of systems, the sensor and control may be combined in a single unit. Similarly, the alarm can be any of a variety of devices. It can be a noisemaker, such as a bell, buzzer, siren, or horn. It can be a warning pilot lamp or a floodlight. Some installations make use of what is known as a silent alarm. Instead of using a noisemaker, the system is connected through a leased telephone line or by a broadcast radio signal to either a police substation or the central office (sometimes called the central station); or to a burglar-alarm company or detective agency that either dispatches guards or calls the police. Unfortunately, central-station alarm systems are not suitable for do-it-yourself installation.

Performance approaching that of a central-station alarm system can be achieved with a self-installed intrusion alarm, if the home ower uses a commercially available instrument known as an automatic telephone dialer. In operation, the instrument is connected to the alarm system and, in case of intrusion, will dial a predetermined number and play a prerecorded message.

Forms of Protection

Depending on its design and installation, an intrusion alarm system may provide for any of several different forms of protection. It may serve, for example, to detect an intruder trying to enter a protected area. Or, the system may respond to an unauthorized person anywhere within the premises or in a specific room. Finally, the system can be designed to respond only if the intruder approaches or touches a specific object, such as a single door, a safe, or a file cabinet. Sometimes a single installation can be set up to furnish two or more forms of protection simultaneously.

Consider the floor plan of a typical small house as shown in the illustration. If an alarm system protects all the doors, windows, and other entrances to the home, or the entire exterior, it is said to offer a perimeter protection. In a physical sense, a fence around a piece of property is perimeter protection. But you can also have perimeter protection in other ways. Flood-

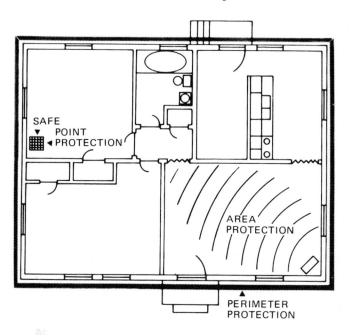

There are three basic forms of protection: perimeter, area, and point. This view shows all three types. (Hydrometals, Inc.)

lights used on the grounds around a house supply perimeter protection. Perimeter protection systems can be used to guard a specific area within a building as well as an entire building, as for example, the entrances to a stock room at a restaurant or bar.

If an alarm system can detect an intruder anywhere in a given area, such as the living room in your home, it provides area protection. You can set up several such systems to protect those rooms containing your valuables, ignoring other rooms, such as bathrooms, kitchen, laundry room, etc. Since area-protection devices can be expensive, using them for a kitchen or bathroom would not only be extravagant, but might become a nuisance. These rooms, and similar rooms, can be used to sound an alarm in a more simple and more economical way.

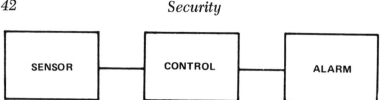

Basic arrangement of an alarm system. The sensor can be any device that responds to a change. A current flows (or stops flowing) to a control, which in turn actuates the alarm. (Speedex Electronics)

Point protection is the protection supplied by an alarm system designed to guard a specific object. For example, you may have a safe at home, or you may have a file cabinet containing valuable papers. You might want to protect these papers even if they were of no worth to anyone else. Not finding anything else of value, a vandal would think nothing of ripping and shredding your papers, and scattering them all over the floor. You can also use point protection to protect large power tools, valuable paintings, cabinets that contain drugs, plan files, and gun cases.

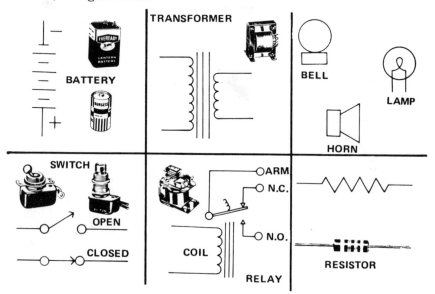

Circuit symbols used by manufacturers of alarm systems. Battery symbol (upper left) is series of short and long parallel lines. Minus and plus symbols are often included, but can be omitted. Transformer (top center) is step-down type and reduces line voltage to 6 to 12 volts AC. Symbols top right are for bell, lamp, and horn. Switches at bottom left are single-pole single-throw type. There are an enormous variety of switches. Any device that opens and closes a circuit can be called a switch. Symbol, bottom center, is a relay. N.C. means normally closed; N.O. means normally open. The arm moving between the upper (N.C.) contact and the lower (N.O.) contact is the armature or switch blade. Resistor (bottom right) limits flow of current in a circuit. (Hydrometals, Inc.)

How Simple Alarm Systems Work

The drawing shows the circuit arrangement of a simple alarm system and is just about as easy to operate as an ordinary doorbell. The alarm device consists of a bell, or a buzzer, or any other gadget that will make a noise. The alarm works when a current of electricity flows through it, but in this arrangement can only happen when the switch is closed. The

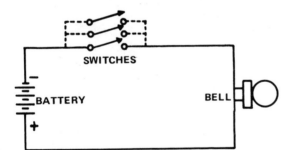

Circuit of a simple alarm system. When any one of the switches is closed, a current will flow from the battery through the alarm, in this case a bell. The switches can be mounted on windows and the door. This is a normally open circuit—that is, current does not flow until one of the switches is pushed to its closed position. (Hydrometals, Inc.)

power source can be a number of dry cells or can be the nearest convenient AC outlet. When you buy the alarm, the manufacturer will supply you with information on just what source of power you should use. You can also get a complete alarm kit containing the switches, batteries, and alarm, plus full instructions on how to wire the system. It is better to do this than to buy the individual components, unless you have had some prior electrical experience. For example, one complete package (On-Guard) is a door-and-window burglar-alarm system that fits all doors and that you can mount in minutes. It is completely self-contained, and is tamper-proof from the outside. It is fully transistorized and has a keyless electronic exit feature with an alarm panic button. The panic button is used to indicate an emergency, or to test the alarm system and the exit button. It is supplied with twenty-five feet of hookup wire, two keys, all the necessary mounting hardware, and operates on a six-volt battery.

Model 618BA

Complete solid-state burglar alarm, closed-circuit system. This kit contains an 8″ alarm bell, electrical switch lock, and a control circuit panel, housed in a heavy duty, weatherproof, steel box that has a built-in tamper-proof circuit. Clipping wires or opening any protected point will cause the alarm to sound. The alarm will continue to sound until it is reset by a key-proof lock switch. This kit includes 4 sets of magnetic door/window switches, 2 keys, warning decals, 100′ of hook-up wire, insulated wiring nails, and mounting hardware. It has an interior on/off switch for setting the alarm system from inside the house, and a test/panic button to indicate an emergency or to test the alarm system. The alarm is powered by a 12-volt lantern battery. (On-Guard)

You can also get combined burglar-alarm and fire-alarm systems to give you double protection. And, while you are now thinking about security, it is a good idea to keep a flashlight in some convenient, easily reachable place near your bed. Should you think you have an intruder in your home, it will be easier and possibly faster to reach for the flashlight than for the light switch. A burglar may also try to get to the powerline junction box in your basement to turn off the main power switch. The reason for doing so would be to deactivate any power-line-operated alarm devices.

Battery-operated alarm systems can be a nuisance in the sense that you must run periodic checks on the system to make sure the battery still supplies power. Even if a battery is not used, it will run down and in time will need to be replaced (if a dry type) or recharged (if a wet type). The advantages, though, of using a batttery is that they seem to outweigh the inconveniences. A battery represents an independent power system. If your AC line voltage fails—and that can happen and has happened—you still have protection. Further, the alarm system cannot be deactivated by an alarm-conscious burglar who makes the fuse box his first stop.

Wired burglar-alarm systems work in a number of ways. Some are closed-circuit types, others use an open circuit. Thus, in an open-circuit type, any attempt by the burglar to clip the connecting wires will set off the alarm. In the closed-circuit type, closing a switch at various protected points will set off the alarm. The point is that the burglar simply does not know what to do.

When installing an alarm system, assuming you buy a complete package, you will receive a number of door and window switches. Sometimes you will have the option (depending on the manufacturer) of buying extra switches, to accommodate your personal needs. The switches are mounted on doors and windows in such a way that the action of opening them would close the switch. This would permit current to flow from the battery to the alarm. These switches could be supplemented by a mat-type switch, placed under a doormat or entrance rug.

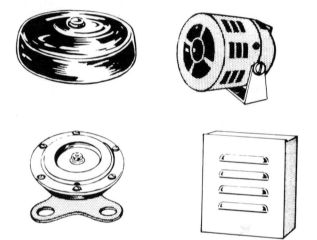

Alarm devices. Top left to right: bell and miniature siren. Bottom left to right: horn and horn cabinet. The siren is best, particularly if it has a changing pitch. If mounted outside, siren should be housed in waterproof enclosure. Wires to siren must be out of reach and require very long stepladder to reach. If possible, siren should face most populated area. (Hydrometals, Inc.)

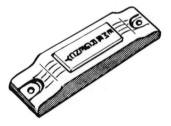

The panic button, also called an emergency button or test button, is an ordinary normally open switch. It can be in many different shapes and sizes. It is used to trip or actuate an alarm system manually. Any number of such switches can be incorporated into an alarm system. Normally, they are wired to the alarm control's normally open sensor terminals using ordinary 2-conductor wiring such as No. 22 or No. 24 gauge alarm, intercom, or speaker wires. The test or panic button can be installed near the front door, in the kitchen or bedroom. Some people prefer putting the panic button on a night table adjacent to the bed since they want the capability of sounding an alarm in case an intruder breaks in. (Hydrometals, Inc.)

When an alarm system of this kind is triggered—that is, turned on—the alarm keeps sounding until a defeat switch is used. The defeat switch is part of the circuit and when operated interrupts the flow of current to the alarm. When mounting the defeat switch, put it in some spot that isn't obvious to an intruder—that is, it should not be out in the open. With an alarm sounding, few burglars will remain on the premises to conduct a search. However, you and the various members of your family should know just where the defeat switch is, and should be able to reach it quickly and easily if the system turns on for any reason.

Slide switch in housing (left) is a general purpose on-off switch useful as an exit/entry alarm switch. The switch at the right is a test- or panic-button type and supplies momentary contact for closed-circuit systems. (On-Guard)

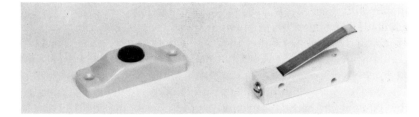

Test- or panic-button (left) can be used to expand an existing alarm system. It supplies momentary contact and is used with open-circuit systems. The unit at the right is an all-purpose switch for sliding doors, windows, and screens. It is used with a closed-circuit system. (On-Guard)

Insulated wiring nails (left). These are used for tacking wires to supporting surfaces, with the wires as part of an alarm system. The units at the right are magnetic door or window switches. They can form part of a closed-circuit-type burglar-alarm system. (On-Guard)

The location of the defeat switch, and as a matter of fact your complete alarm protection system, should not be the subject of discussion. The members of your family should know that the system exists and they should be able to locate the defeat switch in the dark, if necessary. You can be sure that for every alarm system invented, there will always be a burglar somewhere with an ingenious idea for overcoming it.

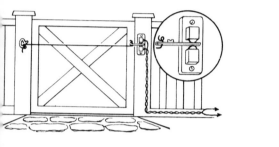

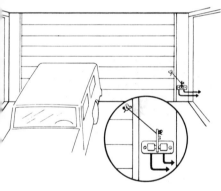

Commercial pull trap and various applications. Various types of
pull traps are made. One consists of a rectangular section of insu-

lating material placed between two spring-loaded bearings. When the insulating material is pulled away, the two metal bearings contact, permitting an electrical current to flow to an alarm system. Drawing A shows a commercial pull trap. Drawing B is a pull trap used to protect a fence gate, while C shows how a pull trap can be used to guard a garage door. With a wire trip cord (drawing D), circuit connections can be made at the ends. In this illustration the pull trap is used to guard a driveway. (Speedex Electronics)

When you buy a commercial alarm system for your home or apartment, you will probably receive a small self-stick label advising that your premises are electronically guarded. Use it. A burglar, noticing the label, may be deterred from trying to enter, and you will be saved the aggravation and expense of replacing broken window and door panes, jimmied locks, and damaged garage doors.

Circuit-System Advantages and Disadvantages

The type of alarm system that uses open switches is identified either as an open-circuit alarm or normally open (NO) system. While it is simple, inexpensive, and effective, it has a number of limitations that reduce its reliability. For example, if one of the wires leading to one of the switches is cut or broken at any point, the alarm will not work. Confronted by such a system, a burglar might be able to cut or snap a wire so quickly that the alarm attracts little or no attention.

The drawing shows the arrangement of a basic closed-circuit alarm system. The thin lines that connect all the parts are wires. If you will trace the wires going from the horn, you will see that one of them is connected to the minus terminal of a battery and that the other wire goes to a switch. This switch is part of a relay.

The various door and window switches shown in the drawing are closed. This means that there is a complete current path from the battery shown at the left, through the switches and through the coil of the relay. This makes the relay into

an electromagnet. The electromagnet keeps the alarm circuit
in an open condition.

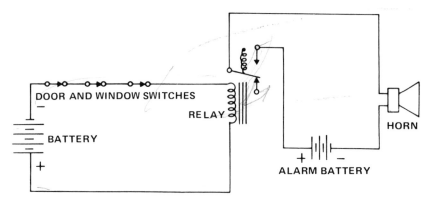

More elaborate alarm system than the one shown on page 000.
This is known as a normally closed system, because the door and
window switches are normally closed. With the arrangement shown
in the drawing, current flows from the battery, through the door
and window switches, and through the coil marked relay. This
flow of current makes the relay coil into an electromagnet. The
magnetism of the relay holds the armature pulled down as shown.
No current can flow from the alarm battery to the horn. If, however, any one of the door or window switches is opened, current
will no longer flow from the battery through the relay coil. The
relay coil will lose its magnetism, and the armature will move to
the upper contact, closing the horn circuit. Current will then flow
from the alarm battery through the horn. (Hydrometals, Inc.)

Now assume that one of the door or window switches opens.
This could be caused by a burglar opening a window or the
door. The current from the battery at the left is interrupted
and so the relay ceases being an electromagnet. The spring
pulls the armature, a sort of switch blade, to the upper contact. Now the circuit to the alarm (a horn, in this case) is
closed, and since current from the alarm battery flows through
the horn, it is activated and sounds an alarm.

This arrangement is more difficult to defeat than the simple
open-circuit arrangement shown earlier. It is generally called
a closed-circuit system, but because a supervisory current flows

through the sensors (the switches) and relay at all times, may be called a supervised system. Since a failure of any part of the sensor circuit (all of the switches) will cause the system to sound an alarm, it can be identified as a fail-safe design.

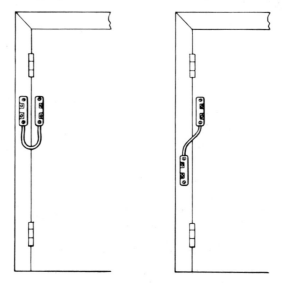

Door cords are two-wire conductor cables that are highly flexible. They are used to provide electrical connections to devices or equipment mounted on hinged access closures such as doors or windows. (Hydrometals, Inc.)

While far superior to the simple open-circuit alarm system, the basic closed-circuit system has a disadvantage of its own. If an open sensor switch is closed, once opened, the system will return to its pre-alarm condition. Thus, an intruder who has accidentally tripped a door or window switch can silence the alarm simply by restoring, or by putting a short across the opened switch. The shorting device can be a short length of copper wire, or it may be a length of wire ending in a pair of spring clips so that the burglar need not hold it, but can clip it into position. Once this is done the burglar can proceed about his business, fully aware now of the type of alarm system confronting him. However, there is a circuit design, as shown in the illustration, which can once again make the burglar's work as perilous as it should be.

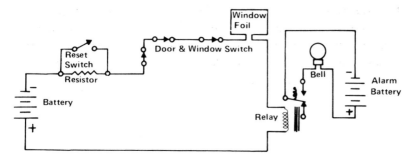

Alarm circuit in which a resistor (a current-limiting device) is used across the reset switch. The resistor limits the current to a value needed to hold the relay closed, but not to close it. If a burglar opens any of the door or window switches, or breaks the window foil, the relay will de-energize, causing the alarm to ring. And the alarm will continue to ring, even if the burglar resets the switch he has opened. This is a much more sophisticated setup than the alarm systems illustrated earlier since it prevents the burglar from silencing the alarm. (Speedex Electronics)

The new circuit is quite similar to the basic closed-alarm system. Several new items have been incorporated, however. One of these is window foil, while the others consist of a reset switch and a resistor. A resistor, shown symbolically by a series of lines that look like sawteeth, is a part that limits or opposes the flow of an electrical current. When the resistor is in the circuit, the amount of current flowing is comparatively small. When the reset switch is closed, it effectively shorts or removes the resistor from the circuit, and so the flow of current is increased.

Electromagnetic relays have an interesting characteristic. They require more current to close their armatures than to hold their armatures in a closed state. In other words, it takes quite a bit of current flowing through the armature coil to make it into a magnet that is sufficiently strong to attract and pull over the armature. But once this is done, once the armature is indeed pulled over, the amount of current needed to hold it in that position is relatively small.

Now, by adding a resistor of the proper value to the circuit, as shown in the illustration, we can limit the supervisory sensor current to the value needed to hold the relay closed, but not to close it, if opened. To close the relay, should it be opened, we short the resistor momentarily by means of the reset switch.

The burglar now has a much tougher circuit to overcome. If he accidentally opens the sensor circuit, by opening a door or any sensor-switch-protected window, the armature of the relay will be pulled away toward the bell-ringing circuit and the alarm will sound. And the alarm will continue to sound, even if he restores a tripped switch or shorts a broken lead. In fact, the only way he can silence the alarm is to either locate and disable the alarm circuit itself, or to locate and operate the reset switch.

The odds are against him, however. The alarm circuit itself can be contained within a strong tamper-proof box, and even if the burglar is able to locate it, and do so quickly, he must work under conditions he always tries to avoid, knowing that the alarm must soon bring someone to investigate. He may also look for the reset switch, but in a well-designed installation, the reset switch itself would be key-operated. The burglar is now faced with a switch that requires a key, and again, picking the lock for the reset switch, or smashing it, or trying

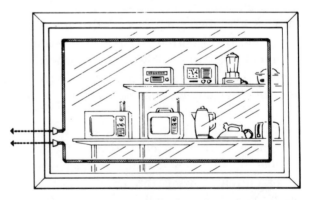

Window foil can be used to protect windows, but is generally used for stores, rather than homes. The foil is a conductor of electrical current. When the foil is torn, as it will be if the window is broken, the flow of current through the foil will be interrupted. As a result, the current through it will stop. It is this stoppage of current flow that triggers the alarm. (Speedex Electronics)

to overcome it would take time, and with the alarm ringing that is just what the burglar does not have. The reset switch can not only be locked, but it can be positioned within a tamper-proof cabinet. Faced with these difficult-to-solve alternatives, the intruder generally will disappear to a less noisy location.

A word about the added window-foil sensor. As shown in the drawing, this is simply a strip of narrow, metallic foil cemented around a glass window and forming a continuous conductive path that can become part of a series electrical circuit. The foil works as a sensor switch. If the window glass is shattered by a burglar trying to enter that way, the foil will be broken, opening the circuit and sounding the alarm.

With such devices available, how is it possible that the number of burglaries is increasing steadily? How is it possible that the number of daytime burglaries is climbing? There are any number of answers.

Roll of window foil. This foil is an electrical conductor. It has a self-adhesive back and is used in closed-circuit systems. Approximately ⅝″ wide, it is used for windows and glass doors. (On-Guard)

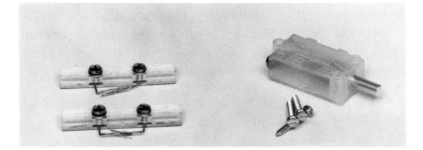

Foil connectors (left) are used for making a wiring connection to
foil used on glass windows and door. These come equipped with a
self-adhesive back for closed-circuit systems. They are very handy
if you want to expand an existing burglar-alarm setup. The unit at
the right is a plunger-type switch for a closed-circuit system, and is
especially designed for casement windows. It has a long override
after contact is made. (On-Guard)

1. Some of the more elaborate alarm systems seem to be
expensive. And while they represent one of the best kinds of
insurance, remember that most people have to be persuaded
into getting insurance.

2. While the owner of a home may have no installation
problems, it is quite another matter for the apartment dweller.
Many leases require that the tenant may not do any wiring in
the apartment, or that if an alarm system is installed, it becomes part of the landlord's property and must remain when
the tenant moves. In many cases the tenant is afraid to inform
the landlord that he wants an alarm system since this could
lead to a demand for a rent increase.

3. Many people have an "it can't happen to me" attitude
and will not consider alarm systems for that reason.

4. Quite a few people have a rather odd notion about our
police departments. Their attitude is that they pay taxes, that
it is the function of the police to protect them, and that if
they are robbed, it must be the fault of the police. Their
common complaint is: "You never see a policeman around
when you need one." Such an attitude is not only childish
and immature, but is completely self-defeating. The only way
—the only possible way—is to acknowledge and realize that

personal security is your job, and that it is a job you must do with the help and cooperation of the police.

5. Quite a few people rely for protection on locks, and then buy the cheapest, poorest-made lock. A good lock is one that has a vertical deadbolt, whose cylinder cannot be pulled out, and is sturdy enough not to be punched out. A good lock is one that requires a key (or some other inserting device) to open it and to close it, and that also has an additional deadbolt operative only from the inside. A good lock is one for which only the home owner or apartment dweller has the key, and it is *not* the lock inherited from the previous occupant. A good lock is one in which the strike is completely covered on the outside. A good lock is mounted on a door so that the edge of the door and its jamb are covered on the outside. A good lock is also mounted on a door whose hinges cannot be removed from the outside. And a good lock is also one that will set off an alarm if it is finally opened by a burglar. A good lock is one that is supplemented by a *strong* key-type chain lock. Unfortunately, many people buy locks on the basis of price. Finally, a good lock is one that is installed by a professional or master locksmith who has been thoroughly advised that security is of paramount importance.

Magnetic Switches

There are many different types of switches, but no matter how they are made, the job they have is the same and that is to open or close a circuit so that an alarm can be sounded. In addition to conventional switches you can buy plunger or pushbutton switches, pull traps, switch mats, window foil, and key switches. There is still another type of switch sensor now popular with intrusion-alarm systems and that is the magnetic switch, as shown in the illustration.

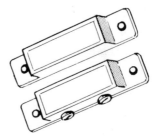

A magnetic switch contains two basic parts: the switch itself and an actuating magnet. (Hydrometals, Inc.)

SWITCH OPEN

SWITCH CLOSED

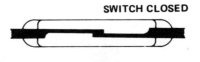

How a magnetic switch works. In the upper drawing the switch is open. The two metal strips inside the switch enclosure do not touch. In the lower drawing a magnet is brought near the switch. The magnet pulls the flexible upper strip down to the fixed lower metal strip. As soon as the contact ends of the two strips touch, the switch is closed. The magnet can be mounted on a door or window, so arranged that movement of the door or window will close the magnetic switch. (Hydrometals, Inc.)

This switch consists of two or more reedlike metallic structures that carry the electrical contacts and are magnetically sensitive. Under normal conditions they are held apart by spring tension. If a magnet is brought near the switch, the reeds snap together, closing the contacts. If the magnet is moved away, spring tension opens the contacts.

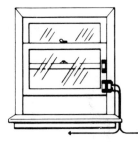

Basic arrangement of magnetic sensors on a window. If window is opened or closed, magnetic sensors detect change of position and switch on alarm. A more secure arrangement is to have the windows additionally protected by foil. (Speedex Electronics)

In practice the magnetic switch is normally mounted on a window or door frame, as shown in the drawing. Wired into a closed-circuit system, the switch will open and trigger an alarm whenever the magnet is moved. Since the magnet is mounted directly on the window frame, the window cannot be opened without moving it. But when this happens, the switch will open and trigger an alarm. Two magnets are provided on the window shown in the drawing to maintain protection whether the window is closed or partially open for ventilation. Either of the two different magnet/switch mounting positions for a door, as shown in the drawing below, is satisfactory for most installations.

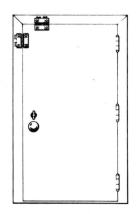

Two possible positions for magnetic switches on a door: anywhere along the top, or the upper portion of the side. This will keep the switch out of the reach of young fingers. Two switches are shown here to indicate alternate locations—only one switch is needed for a door. The wiring to the switch can be tacked into place with insulating wiring nails. (Hydrometals, Inc.)

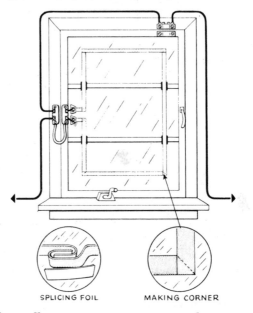

SPLICING FOIL   MAKING CORNER

Window-foil installation using magnetic switch sensors for the upper and lower windows. The insert at the left shows the method for splicing the foil. The inset at the right indicates the correct method for making a foil corner. The heavy black lines (terminated in arrows) represent the wires leading away from the sensors. (Hydrometals, Inc.)

Electronic vs. Electrical Systems

A completely wired alarm system is an electrical type. And that is one of the difficulties of such a system. It requires long wires and these wires must be thick enough to carry the amount of current needed by the system. The wires must be concealed as much as possible, not only from an esthetic point of view, but to make it as difficult as possible for the burglar to be able to locate and disable them.

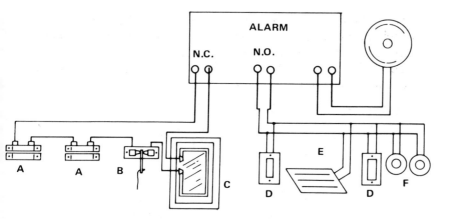

Alarm systems can be arranged in many different ways, depending on which and how many entry areas are to be protected, and on the amount of room area and point protection wanted. The letter A represents a pair of magnetic switches that can be used on doors and windows. B is a pull trap for guarding a road, driveway, or path. C shows a normally closed window-foil installation. D is a normally open test/panic button. E is a switch-type mat, often placed right before the door on the inside, or at the foot of steps. The letter F represents a pair of fire sensors. (Hydrometals, Inc.)

An electronic system is one that depends on a radio wave or a supersonic wave, a wave whose pitch is so high that human beings cannot hear it. Modern electronic systems use space-age devices such as transistors, silicon-controlled rectifiers, infrared sensors, integrated circuits, ceramic transducers, and microwave antennas.

Electronic systems can be grouped into two basic categories: those that require the burglar to make physical contact with a sensor device or something to which the sensor is attached—that is, he must pull open a door, open or break a window, step on a switch mat. The other types of electronic alarms are those that require no physical contact for they can detect an intruder when he interrupts a beam of light, just enters a certain area, makes a sound, or just moves about.

Photoelectric Burglar Alarms

Photoelectric burglar alarms were among the first to utilize electronic circuits. Popularly called an electric eye, the basic photoelectric system consists of a light source and a light-sensitive detector similar to the elements used in ordinary photographic exposure meters. The detector can be coupled to an amplifier and either a solid state or electromagnetic relay. In operation, a change in the light falling on the detector (or sensor) will actuate the alarm. Thus, a burglar stepping into the light beam and interrupting it would cause the alarm to sound.

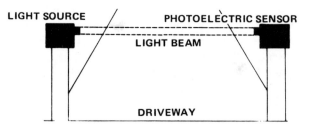

Protection of a driveway by photoelectric method. Light source sends beam of light to photoelectric sensor. If light beam is interrupted, sensor helps trigger an alarm. (Speedex Electronics)

This is an extremely versatile alarm system and can be used in a number of applications. You can use it, for example, to detect unauthorized entry to your private driveway by putting a light source on one side of the road and the sensor on the opposite side, as shown in the illustration. Here the light beam will be interrupted by an approaching vehicle. A similar arrangement can be used to guard a gate, door, or window, or even a whole line of doors or windows, as along one side of a hallway or building.

Two or more photoelectric systems, together with mirrors, can be used to set up a "light fence" around an enclosure or a home affording complete perimeter protection.

Photoelectric systems can also be adapted to supply area and point protection. The illustration shows a technique in which mirrors are used to crisscross a light beam back and forth across an entire area. If the light beam is interrupted at any point, the alarm will go off. You can get point protection by directing a light beam at a mirror attached to the protected object, such as the door of a safe, and using the photoelectric sensor to pick up the reflected light. Anyone standing in front of the object or moving his hand directly toward it will trip the alarm.

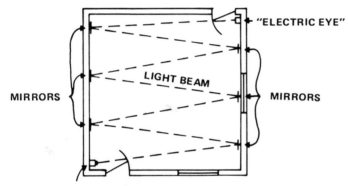

LIGHT SOURCE

Photoelectric technique for area protection. A light beam is produced by a light source and is bounced back and forth by mirrors until it reaches the electric eye. Any interruption of any part of the light beam will trigger the alarm. If the light source fails, or the mirrors get dirty (reducing their reflectivity), or the electric eye fails, the system turns on. (Speedex Electronics)

Some photoelectric systems use visible light, while others work with invisible infrared light. During the daytime it may be difficult for a burglar to see the visible light beam, but the infrared beam is much more difficult to detect and defeat. The simpler systems can be defeated by using an ordinary flashlight as a substitute light. The burglar, generally with the help of an accomplice, keeps his flashlight pointed at the sensor, and as long as this is done, the alarm will not go off. A simple metal stand to hold the flashlight firmly in position can be used, so that the burglar is certain that the alarm will not be tripped. To defeat the burglar, one technique is to use an interrupted light beam with the electronic circuit designed to respond only to such a source. The light pulses can be made to occur so swiftly that to the burglar the beam is a steady one. However, any attempt to use a substitute steady light source, such as a flashlight, including an infrared flashlight, will trip the alarm. Even if the burglar is aware that the beam is an interrupted type, he has no way of knowing if the light pulses are all uniform, or how often they occur.

A few manufacturers offer photoelectric security alarms that do not require specific light sources. Providing area protection, they monitor the average light level in the guarded area, serving to detect changes in the absorption or reflection of background light as a result of the movement of an intruder. If there is a sudden change in average light intensity, caused by an intruder using a flashlight or switching on a light, or even by the intruder's shadow falling across a normally bright area, the system will detect the change and set off the alarm.

Lamps can be turned on and off automatically by photoelectric switch. During daytime hours photoelectric switch receives light from outside and keeps lamp turned off. At dusk, in absence of light, photoelectric switch turns lamp on. The disadvantage is that the light remains on all night, not a usual or normal lighting sequence in a home. A better arrangement is to have several timers that turn lights on and off in various parts of the house or apartment, but that turn off completely at some more usual hour, such as one or two o'clock in the morning. (Speedex Electronics)

The Capacity Alarm

A pair of metal plates, separated by air, or some other insulating material such as mica, is known as a capacitor. When the capacitor is connected to a source of voltage, such as a battery, the capacitor will become electrically charged. The amount of charge depends on the area of the metal plates, how close the plates are to each other, and the material between the plates. If, for example, you bring your fingers close to the capacitor plates, the electrical charge on those plates will change. There is no need to touch the plates; the proximity of your fingers is enough.

This phenomenon is used in another type of electronic alarm system, which senses changes in the electrical charge on a metal plate as a person approaches. Known as capacity alarms, these systems are often used for point protection. There are some sophisticated versions available that use long wires instead of plates—the basic idea of a charge on a plate remains the same—and that can supply excellent perimeter protection.

Sound and Vibration Alarms

Another type of electronic alarm system is one that responds to a sound. The simplest uses a sensitive microphone as a sensor, with the microphone connected to a high-gain audio amplifier similar for those used in hi-fi systems. Others use special vibration sensors similar to the 'tilt' detectors in pinball machines. When adjusted for maximum sensitivity, the vibration detector can pick up a soft padded footstep across a room of fair size.

The trouble with sound and vibration alarm systems is that they can produce frequent false alarms. Thus, the passage of a heavy truck can cause a vibration-type alarm to go off.

Ultrasonic Alarms

The ultrasonic alarm is one of the most effective of the modern electronic intrusion-detection systems. The ultrasonic system uses air vibrations similar to those emitted by "silent" dog whistles, whistles that produce sound outside the range of human hearing.

In operation, an ultrasonic alarm system radiates a very high frequency or ultrasonic signal into the protected area with the help of a special type of loudspeaker. It then detects the echoes that bounce back to it. The pitch of the echo is compared electronically with the original ultrasonic wave sent out by the loudspeaker. Under normal conditions, both sounds, the original and the echo, will be identical. Should there be a moving object within the area, such as an intruder, the echoes will be changed. This difference will be detected and will serve as a control signal to set off the alarm.

ULTRASONIC ALARM

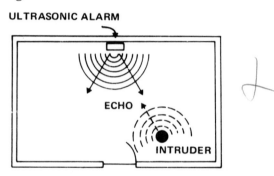

How an ultrasonic alarm works. Ultrasonic generator radiates inaudible waves, covering selected area. Intruder steps into wave area, causing ultrasonic echo to go back to sensor. Sensor actuates alarm. (Speedex Electronics)

Capable of extreme sensitivity and ideal for area protection, ultrasonic alarm systems suffer from one limitation: They will respond to any movement, even air movement, within their range. As a result, pets and children must be kept out of the area. Fans and blasts of air from an air conditioner, can also set off the alarm.

The operation of an ultrasonic space alarm is based on a law of physics known as the Doppler principle. This principle states that if there is movement within an area of sound waves, the movement will change these sound waves at a given rate. This change and rate can be sampled and detected. If the change is such that it would be caused by human movement, the control unit is set into an alarm condition. If the change is caused by any other turbulence in the area, it would be filtered out without causing alarm.

7-2 ULTRASONIC WAVES SENSE INTRUSION WITHIN A CONE-SHAPED AREA, AS SHOWN ABOVE.

Ultrasonic waves are invisible and inaudible. They radiate from an ultrasonic generator somewhat like a beam of light, forming a cone-shaped area. Intrusion into this area sets off the alarm. The ultrasonic generator can be positioned to cover a door, windows (possible entry points), or valuable objects within a room. (Speedex Electronics)

One sound system fills an area with sound energy at 20.2 KHz (20.2 thousand cycles per second), a frequency above human hearing. This is done by mounting a transmitter in the area to be protected. In the same area a receiver is mounted to detect the continuous 20.2-KHz signal. The detected signal is sent to the control unit, where both frequency and amplitude are sampled. Human movement will change the 20.2-KHz signal by approximately 40 Hz (40 cycles per second), depending on the movement. This 40-cycle change will cause an alarm condition. Any other movement, such as swaying curtains, window rattling, etc. will change the 20.2-KHz signal appreciably above or below the 40-cycle rate, and thus have no effect on the alarm system.

Combined Protection

An alarm system is not a substitute for locks nor are locks an alternative for alarms. Both are needed if you want maximum security. Whether you should have both depends on individual requirements. If you live in an apartment that is in a very low crime-rate area, and if the lobby is security-guard protected, and if you have had a pair of front-door locks installed by a master locksmith, then you might consider your protection adequate. If you have a home with substantial amounts of silverware, jewelry, and furs, then what is sufficient for an apartment may not be enough for you. The purpose of a lock is to keep a burglar out; the object of an alarm system is to stop the burglary and/or to apprehend the burglar.

Where to Put the Sensor Switches

Most often sensor switches are installed on the door or doorjamb or on one or more windows. But these are precisely the areas that burglars expect you to install switches and so an experienced burglar may work out some technique for defeating them. Security in the home is an unending battle between those who want to break and enter and the homeowner who wants to keep burglars out.

There are many places in the home you can install switches for the purpose of turning on an alarm. One company, Tapeswitch Corp. of America, manufactures Flexswitch, a flexible switch in ribbon form. You can use this remarkable switch under the padding of a chair. A burglar momentarily resting from his labors will set off an alarm if he does so. This same switch put into draperies will detect entry when the seams are flexed. You can put the switch under the mattress in a bed, or just

Flexible switch has numerous security applications. It can be sewn in draperies, mounted under chairs, or behind pictures. It may be undetected by thief because it doesn't resemble ordinary switches. (Tapeswitch Corp.)

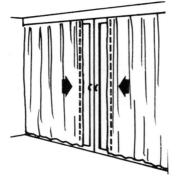

Flexible strip switches can be mounted in draperies. Detects entry when seams are flexed. (Tapeswitch Corp.)

lay it across a doorknob. The simple act of turning the doorknob in either direction will actuate the switch. You can put the
switch behind valuable oil paintings so that any movement of
the picture will ring an alarm. You can mount such switches
in drawers that contain valuables, or arrange the switch so that
moving a safe will cause an alarm. And, finally, you can even
protect the dog who is supposed to protect you by putting in a
switch for him as well.

Flexible switch or strip-type switch can be mounted behind valuable painting. Movement of painting turns on device that signals
alarm. (Tapeswitch Corp.)

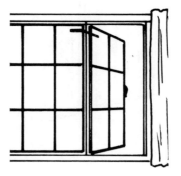

Flexible switch can be used for overhang, casement, or basement
windows. (Tapeswitch Corp.)

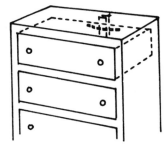

Switch can be installed in one or more drawers. Opening any drawer that is protected this way will start alarm. (Tapeswitch Corp.)

Switch can be imbedded in any cushioning material. Burglar sitting in chair or using it to hold anything will trigger alarm. (Tapeswitch Corp.)

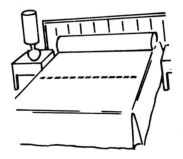

Even a bed can be wired to signal an alarm. If burglar throws any object on the bed, switch will turn on alarm. This kind of switch can be effective because it is so unusual. (Tapeswitch Corp.)

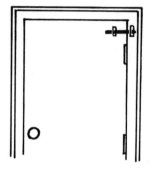

The opening of a door can operate a switch to set off an alarm. (Tapeswitch Corp.)

One method of point protection. Safe is mounted on wheels. If safe is moved out of position, switch is actuated, setting off an alarm. (Tapeswitch Corp.)

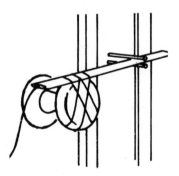

The doorknob switch. Turning the doorknob in either direction actuates the switch. (Tapeswitch Corp.)

Alarm Timing

Generally, if an alarm rings in a house, a burglar will try to make his getaway in as few seconds as possible. However, since the alarm has been set off, it will continue to blast until someone stops it. Since the alarm has achieved its purpose, there is no point in having it blast continuously. Some alarm systems do just that, but others have an on-off cycle. Some alarm systems have automatic timing, with a certain amount of time on, then a certain amount of time off, enough to give you the time to reach the defeat switch. With some alarms, the timing is built in and you cannot change it. With others, you can set the alarm timing any way you want.

With an alarm system in the house it would be advisable to notify your nearest friendly neighbor just what the system is and show where the defeat switch is located. It would also be a good idea to take your local police into your confidence.

Police Alarm

With our current statistics and the rate at which they are mounting, you have every reason to be concerned for your safety and you should do everything within your power to ensure it. But not everyone cares to have an alarm system in his home. An alarm can frighten the occupant of a home about as much as a burglar. Some alarms are so loud and so insistent that they can even scare home owners who know about them and who can anticipate the sound. And some people find an alarm a traumatic shock. There is little doubt that elderly people and those with heart conditions may suffer. The solution is the use of a telephone alarm, such as the type manufactured by American Telephone Alarm Systems. The telephone alarm can be programmed to respond to any emergency condition. It is an automatic telephone reporting device that communicates emergency information by prerecorded tape to the proper authorities. The minute an intruder tampers with any protected opening in your home, the telephone alarm instantly telephones the police, automatically calls for help, and gives the exact location of the emergency. The telephone alarm is a compact telephone communicator that operates on regular house current. It will automatically switch over to a built-in battery standby unit in the event of a power failure, thus insuring continuous operation under all power conditions. For each forced entry, the telphone alarm will make three or more separate phone calls. However, it does not interfere with the regular use of your telephone, as it is directly connected into special equipment supplied to you by your local telephone company.

How to Position Intruder Alarms

If you decide to install an intruder alarm of the radar-wave or ultrasonic type, then you must come to some decision about the area you want to cover. For example, the pattern of the alarm may not cover the entire floor or room. However, in most cases, a single, properly situated intruder alarm is capable of safeguarding you effectively. If you have selected an ultra-

An unexpected light, turned on by a timer, or an alarm, indoors or out, is often enough to deter the amateur burglar.

sonic type of alarm, consider these possibilities as "burglar-trap zones."

1. Hallways or corridors connecting one section of your home with another. If a burglar is to get something out of your home, he will need to move from one room to the next, unless he is already thoroughly familiar with the layout and has already made a prior decision about what he wants to steal.

2. Stairways.

3. Areas with exterior openings that offer possible entrance for burglars.

Be certain that the burglar-trap zone is within the wave pattern of your alarm system. Don't select areas where small children or pets can enter the trap zone and cause false alarms.

Don'ts of Intruder Alarm Installations

Intruder alarms often come equipped with a sensitivity control. Do not advance this control—that is, make the unit extremely sensitive. If you do, you will find you will have a number of false alarms. Don't use the intruder alarm in rooms

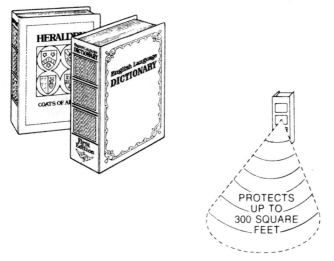

An ultrasonic alarm system concealed in a book. The waves generated by the ultrasonic generator can protect up to 300 square feet, with a teardrop-shaped pattern depending on environmental conditions. Any significant motion occurring within this pattern will cause the alarm to respond. When motion is first detected, a lamp or other appliance connected to the unit will turn on immediately. Seconds later, the internal alarm and/or the optional external alarm horn will sound. The appliance and the alarm remain on as long as the intruder is present and for approximately one minute after motion has stopped. Then the alarm and appliance turn off, and the unit automatically resets itself, supplying continuous coverage. (3M Co.)

with open windows. Don't permit children or pets to enter an area when the intruder alarm is switched to the alarm position. Don't use an intruder alarm outdoors.

Some intruder alarm systems do a double job. They not only sound an alarm, but turn on a light when the protected area is entered. In one arrangement the intrusion alarm system is disguised as a book that hides its presence. It is a completely self-contained solid-state circuit and can be installed anywhere that an electric outlet is available. And it turns on a buzzer and selected lights at thirty-second intervals.

The Add-On System

When homes or apartments are located in high-crime areas, it may be difficult or expensive to get property insurance. In some cases insurance becomes available only after the resident agrees to install some type of alarm system. Some alarm systems are being designed for "add-on" capabilities, so you can begin with a starter system and then gradually add more and more protection. The advantage here is that you will get some basic protection, and you will be able to buy a system that is within your budget. And then you can add on more sensor switches, or have greater area coverage when you can afford to do so. And if you are building a new home, you should know that some building contractors are now including alarm systems as an option. One of the advantages of doing so during construction is that it is much easier to install concealed wiring before walls are erected.

The Lock Alarm

Probably one of the simplest alarm systems is the alarm that forms part of a front-door lock. 3M has a lock alarm it calls the Outkeeper. This unit is a lock alarm that combines all the features of a quality deadbolt lock, plus a self-contained battery-operated pre-entry burglar alarm. The pre-entry alarm helps scare intruders away before they break in. Any attempts to force the door, force the chain (the lock comes equipped with a chain), or pull the cylinder will trigger the alarm. The lock has a heavy duty one-inch bolt with a saw-proof pin. Any efforts to force the bolt will set off the alarm.

Window Jammers

According to the FBI, burglars, vandals, and other intruders break into over 2 million American homes every year. A determined invader gets in through doors, windows—any and all openings in your home. And the rising crime rate shows that it takes more than just locks on your doors to stop these break-in artists. This means that your windows must also be protected, and this applies equally to upstairs windows, basement casement windows, and garage windows, as well as to ground or main-floor windows. There are any number of devices that can be fastened to windows that will make the burglar's job a more difficult one. Windows usually come equipped with a center latch, but this latch is inadequate for a number of reasons. It only works when the windows are completely shut and so it is ineffective during the warmer months. Also, when the interior window frame is painted, the latch is often painted over and so it gradually freezes in the open position. Further, it can be opened by any burglar who wants to go to the slight trouble of breaking a window or cutting it open.

There are a number of window-locking supplements, generally available in hardware stores. One is a screw type, while another is a thumb-operated type that works by depressing it at one end. Both of these lock the upper and lower window together. The advantage is that these devices permit the window to be opened any amount and still supply a locking feature. But they have the disadvantage that they can be opened by any burglar who can remove a windowpane. Other window-protective devices include the window jammer. This wedge-shaped device is usually mounted on the upper right-hand side of a window a few inches above the center bar. In the closed or locked position, the unit will block and stop any attempt to open either the top or bottom window. However, it can also be defeated by any burglar getting past the window glass.

Another type of window-protective device comes with a lock. But it does get to be a nuisance, particularly if you have a large number of windows and must go around locking each one. A keyed window lock, though, does give more protection than the ordinary screw or snap in position type.

As mentioned earlier, you can use window foil as a sensor for the window to set off an alarm in the event the window is broken. However, foil is quite conspicuous and if your home décor is important to you, then it would give you protection with dissatisfaction. You can get a window sensor that doesn't use foil. Known as the wireless Window Bug (Phillips Enterprises), it is designed specifically for windows. It consists of a small electronic device that senses shock from breaking windows and is wired directly to a transmitter. The Bug mounts easily on any window glass with adhesive backing that is supplied and can be externally adjusted for sensitivity. No separate power supply is required as the Window Bug is powered by the battery in the transmitter. One Window Bug will protect up to a hundred square feet of glass such as a 10′ × 10′ pane. There are no false alarms caused by knocking on the glass with bare knuckles or by tapping the glass with a key or coin and it is not vibration-sensitive.

There are various kinds of switches made for windows for use in connection with window alarm systems, including those having contacts of the magnetic, leaf, or button types.

You might think that a burglar would hesitate to break a window but consider that, unlike a door, windows supply a burglar with a choice. He does not need to select a window that is near an outside light, but can choose one that is at the rear of the home and hidden from view. And a burglar can break a pane of glass without making much sound, if any. All he does is to run tape over the window and then tap the glass with a tool. The glass breaks but doesn't fall. The burglar then pulls the tape away and the glass comes with it.

The Alarm

If you are going to have an alarm in your home or apartment, you quite naturally do not want any device that is so large and so conspicuous that it interferes with your decoration scheme. You can get one that is quite small, the Tone-Alert, a miniature electronic audible warning device. Attractively housed in molded plastic, this alarm unit measures

Not all alarms are large. This inconspicuous, attractively packaged alarm is less than 2″ across. There is nothing small about the sound it produces, though. (Tone Alert, MRL, Inc.)

1″ in diameter by ¹¹⁄₁₆″ high with ⁵⁄₁₆″ plastic over metal flanges for mounting. The alarm is solid-state for long life.

Simple Door or Window Alarms

There are numerous inexpensive alarm devices available but such gadgets are often not worth the room they take up. Not only do they have extremely limited use, but they may instill a false sense of security, depriving the house owner or apartment dweller of adequate protection. One such gimmick is the simple door or window alarm, usually completely self-contained in a thin plastic box and powered by Penlite cells. Such cells aren't really designed for this purpose, have a short life, and require frequent replacement.

Devices of this kind shouldn't really masquerade under the heading of alarms, for they are really annunciators and are simply a modified form of door buzzer, now doing double duty as an alleged alarm system.

These bargain basement alarms sound their buzzer when a door or window is opened, but stop just as soon as either one is closed again. They do serve some purpose, for example, as a bedroom-door alarm (as explained earlier in Chapter 2) or in a small shop to alert the proprietor that someone has entered a rear or front door. You can also use them on your house doors to alert you when children come or go. As far as security is concerned, you can put one or more on your bedroom windows to wake you should a burglar try to make entry that way. The weak sound produced by the buzzer shouldn't be considered as having deterrent value.

A better arrangement is to buy a window alarm made by a manufacturer in the security field. One of these is the Magna-Sentry (Hydrometals, Inc.), a self-contained, battery-operated burglar and fire alarm intended for the point protection of doors, windows, and other access openings. Suitable for apartments, business offices, campers, toolsheds, field offices, etc., the device can be installed without tools in a minute and easily moved to another location when necessary. Since it is relatively inexpensive, you can protect a large number of windows and doors with it.

The Magna-Sentry has many of the features of more expensive professional alarm systems. It has a transistorized latching circuit that is activated by a magnetic switch and also has a built-in heat (fire) sensor that will sound the alarm when the temperature reaches 135 degrees Fahrenheit. This latter feature operates at all times, even if the unit is turned off.

In operation the device sounds a loud warning signal that can penetrate throughout the average house, apartment, or office whenever the protected window or door is opened just an inch or two. Once activated, the alarm will continue to

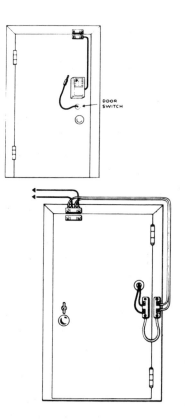

sound until the batteries are exhausted, or until switched off with the special key supplied with the unit. It cannot be silenced just by reclosing the protected door or window.

An accessory door (key) switch is available that, when installed, will let you leave and enter the protected premises without activating the alarm yourself. You can mount the Magna-Sentry either on or next to a door, as shown in the illustrations. You can also use it on double-hung sash and casement windows. The device is supplied with a pressure-sensitive adhesive back, or it can be more permanently installed with wood screws.

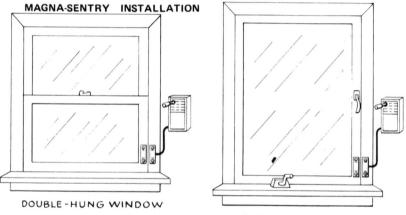

MAGNA-SENTRY   INSTALLATION

DOUBLE-HUNG WINDOW

CASEMENT WINDOW

Magna-Sentry installation on double-hung window (left) or on casement window (right). (Hydrometals, Inc.)

For correct operation, the switch and magnet should be as close as possible, but not rub. Any separation distance up to $\frac{3}{16}''$ is good. The Magna-Sentry requires two size "D" flashlight cells. While any type can be used, alkaline cells are best and should supply up to two years of service, if you buy fresh cells. Conventional zinc-carbon batteries, depending on quality and age, should last three to nine months. The Magna-Sentry doesn't use current unless the alarm is activated, so battery life is equivalent to the cell's normal shelf life, or the time required for natural chemical deterioration.

The Alarm Problem

Installing an alarm system and then hoping for the best isn't enough. If the alarm is indoors it may not be heard if the alarm isn't loud enough and if all windows and doors are closed, as they probably are. A better arrangement is to have an inside and outside alarm, a step that is easier to take with a house than an apartment. But even with an apartment the possibility exists that the owner of the building might permit the use of an outdoor alarm.

Many alarm signaling devices go unnoticed because of their steady, monotonous sound. The best arrangement is a siren sound that changes its pitch, something a bell-ringing alarm is unable to do. And a cycled alarm with a varying pitch is still better. This means the alarm will have an on-off sequence. You can add an outboard module that will vary the pitch and cycle of an alarm but this adds to the cost. That is why some alarm systems cost more than others—they supply more. It may be more expensive to buy an alarm system and then add outboard components to it than to purchase the best system the first time.

Horn Ratings

Horns are rated in terms of their voltage and current requirements by the amount of input power, and by their sound output in decibels (dB). Current to a horn can range from a fraction of an ampere to several amperes. Horn voltage is either 6 volts or 12 volts DC, but some are also designed to work from the 115-volt AC-power line.

The DC-power input to a horn is the product of the voltage and current going to it—that is, the amount of current in amperes multiplied by the amount of voltage in volts. If a horn takes 1 ampere of current at 6 volts, then its DC-power input is $1 \times 6 = 6$ watts. The greater the power input to a horn, the louder it will sound.

When two or more horns are used, they are connected in parallel. The total power used is the sum of the individual powers of the horns. If you connect two 6-watt horns together, their total power operating requirement will be 12 watts. Since the voltage of the battery connected to the horns does not change, the greater the number of horns, the larger the amount of current flowing to them. Thus, if you have two horns connected to a 6-volt battery, with each requiring 1 ampere of current, the total current will be 2 amperes. $2 \times 6 = 12$ watts. If the horns are identical, each will have an operating power of 6 watts.

The wires connecting the horns to the horn battery must be capable of carrying the required current. The amount of current will depend on the number of horns you use. If you use four horns, with each calling for 0.5 ampere of current, then $4 \times 0.5 = 2$ amperes. The connecting wire must be capable of carrying this amount of current. The current-carrying capability of wire depends on its cross-sectional area, with the length of the wire having some effect on the total current the wire can carry. The thicker the wire, the more current it can handle. The longer the wire, the greater the resistance or opposition of the wire to the flow of current. Before buying wire for an alarm system, then, you should know how much current each alarm will require and the total length of wiring required. The total length is twice the distance from the battery to the alarm since you must have one wire from the battery to the alarm and another from the alarm to the battery. If the battery is 20 feet from the alarm, you will need a minimum of 40 feet of wire. Make allowance for the fact that the wire will usually not be connected in a straight line between the battery and the alarm.

The Alarm Battery

The voltage of an alarm battery is fixed, and can be 6 volts, 12 volts, or some other value. The horn rating must match the voltage rating of the battery. Thus, you would use a 6-volt horn with a 6-volt battery, a 12-volt horn with a 12-volt battery.

The current-delivering ability of a battery is rated in ampere hours, and is an indication of the number of amperes a battery can deliver over a period of time. A 20-ampere-hour battery, for example, can theoretically supply 1 ampere for 20 hours or 2 amperes for 10 hours, or 4 amperes for 5 hours. The ampere-hour rating isn't precise since horns, bells, and sirens aren't usually operated over long periods of time. The larger the ampere-hour rating of a battery, the heavier it will usually be, and the more it will cost.

Batteries don't last forever, but are self-consuming, and so their current-delivering capacity constantly decreases. This is a very slow process, so a good plan is to try the test button about once a week just to make sure the alarm system is operative. If the alarm goes on but the tone seems to become noticeably weaker as the sound is prolonged, the usual trouble is a weak battery. If you are using a rechargeable type of battery, you can bring it up to operating condition by connecting it to a charger. It's a good idea to put a battery on charge for a short time, about a half-hour or so, at least once a week. It is possible to determine the state of charge of a battery with a voltmeter, but to do so the alarm must be connected and working. If the battery voltage has decreased by 20 percent it is time for a recharge. Thus, if a 6-volt battery measures somewhat less than 5 volts, you should recharge it. To make the test use a DC voltmeter, with the plus lead of the meter (usually a red-coded lead) connected to the plus terminal of the battery and the minus lead (usually coded black) to the minus terminal of the battery. You must turn on the system—that is, the alarm, siren, or bell must be operating—during the voltage measurement. You can do this by pushing the test/panic button of the system. A voltage measurement without the horn blasting will be meaningless since you will probably find that under such test conditions the battery will indicate full voltage. Of course, if the system uses two or more sirens, possibly one inside and the other out, both should be on during the voltage test.

Chapter 4

Bunco

Every crime requires two persons: the perpetrator and the victim. Even if the victim is not present at the crime, it is his cooperation that makes the crime possible. The smaller the extent of cooperation, the less likely it is that the crime will reach a successful conclusion. An unlocked car door, an apartment with inadequate locks, careless walking at night through heavy crime areas—these are all examples of cooperation that invite crime.

There are two types of cooperation, active and passive. In passive cooperation, the thief tries to avoid confrontation with the victim. Someone who steals the tires off your car is probably appreciative that you parked your car in a dark area next to a vacant lot, but he would be less appreciative if you made an appearance while he was at work.

A crime in which there is active cooperation is called by

various names, bunco, scam, or confidence among them. Many
crimes of this type are based on a well-known but highly
prevalent human failing, the desire to make money without
working for it. There is a saying that we all have some larceny
in us. It is this larcenous streak that makes us susceptible to
bunco-related crimes. Oddly enough, many of these crimes
are designated as "games," such as the Bank Game, Badger
Game, Easy Money Game, etc.

Pigeon Drop

There is no racism in crime, nor is crime restricted by virtue
of creed, nationality, age, or sex. Criminals can be of any age,
any color, male or female, be citizens or aliens, and can have
any religion or no religion.

Pigeon drop is generally operated by females, either white
or black, or operating interracially. The victims of this bunco
game are usually elderly women and can be women of any
race.

Although this bunco has many variations, it generally ad-
heres to the following guidelines: The victim is selected in a
bank or an above-average neighborhood. The first bunco operator, appearing quite sociable, engages the victim in conversation. At this time the second bunco operator appears on
the scene and finds an envelope on the floor. The first operator
calls the attention of the victim to the find.

The finder of the envelope, the second operator, opens it
and is startled to find that the envelope apparently contains
a large sum of money. Since this game is played out in the
direct presence of the victim and her newly found friend,
there is no way in which the envelope's finder can disguise
or hide her newly acquired riches. Consequently, she approaches the victim and the first bunco operator, and says:
"You saw me find this envelope, didn't you? It doesn't have
any name on it. Look! It must have eight or nine thousand
dollars in it. What in the world are *we* going to do with it?"

Note the word *we*. It is with the use of this single word

that the bunco operator ties all three of them together. And now the victim begins to rationalize mentally; she was present at the find, her presence was acknowledged, and "finders are keepers" becomes an acceptable philosophy.

Now the two operators start a discussion about various ways of handling the money. At this time, one of the bunco operators suggests that they contact her employer, an attorney. She is certain there would be no legal fee, for she is a long-time trusted employee. The three women then proceed to an impressive looking office building where the "employee" takes an elevator to an upper floor, leaving the two other women waiting for her in the lobby. Shortly thereafter she returns and states that her employer counted the contents of the envelope and found that the amount was twelve thousand dollars, and that the three women were legally entitled to it in the absence of any known or rightful owner. However, as far-fetched as this might seem, the "attorney" requested that each of the sharers of this new fortune prove their financial responsibility to him, commensurate with the amount of their expected share.

The first operator immediately states that she has four thousand dollars as proof of her financial responsibility, and offers the money to be shown to her fictitious employer.

Attention then shifts to the victim to show proof of her financial responsibility. Reluctantly, the victim produces her bankbook showing a balance in excess of the required amount. However, because bankbooks are easily acquired and altered, the victim is persuaded to go back to the bank to withdraw the required amount. Thereafter, the three go back to the lobby of the office building to wait while the alleged attorney examines each person's offering of financial responsibility.

To ensure the honesty of each of the three women, the twelve thousand dollars have been sealed in the original envelope and entrusted to the care of the victim. With the trap set, the first bunco operator gives her purported four thousand dollars to the second bunco operator for examination. Shortly thereafter, the second operator returns and states that her employer agrees that she should share in the proceeds of the found money.

The moment of truth has arrived. The victim now gives her four thousand dollars to the second bunco operator as evidence of her financial responsibility.

Now you may think the victim is naïve in parting with four thousand dollars, but consider what has just happened. She has just seen the first operator hand the second operator that same amount to demonstrate her financial responsibility. Also, she is being trusted, for she now has in her hands an envelope containing twelve thousand dollars. And so she turns over her money to operator number two, who promptly disappears into an elevator with it, presumably to show her employer.

The two women, the victim and the first bunco operator, remain in the lobby, but as time passes, the bunco operator becomes fidgety and lets her discomfort be seen. Finally, she suggests to the victim that she wait in the lobby, while she (the operator) looks for her friend. She, too, disappears into the elevator.

The victim is now alone in the lobby, but she still has the envelope. Finally, afer waiting for a long time, she slits open the envelope, only to find that it contains nothing but rectangular slips of newspaper.

A pigeon drop is sometimes called a switch and, of course, there are many variations. The victim is the pigeon. If the pigeon had insisted on immediately reporting the find to the nearest police station, the two bunco operators, working in collusion, would have found some good reason to disappear and to search for a less honest victim.

In the pigeon drop, the two bunco operators make every effort to determine the amount the victim has on deposit in her bank. If it turns out that she has no funds, or if she has no immediate access to a substantial amount of cash, the operators find some pretext for leaving, taking their loaded envelope with them.

This bunco game is played on women because women, presumably, are less sophisticated in money matters than men. However, this does not mean that men are immune to bunco, for our built-in tendency to larceny applies to both sexes.

If the bunco operators are caught, the value of the property taken determines whether they will be charged with grand larceny or petty theft.

Jamaican Switch

The Jamaican switch is a form of theft perpetrated by two male blacks against men of all races and all ages. One of the operators approaches the victim, on the street, on a bus or subway, or in a store, and, assuming a foreign accent, informs the victim that he is a sailor and is looking for a particular hotel. The name of the hotel he supplies is fictitious. At this time the second bunco artist walks by, stops for a moment, and then joins in the conversation. The first bunco operator now asks the victim to inquire about the hotel from the second bunco operator, indicating he is looking for that particular hotel because there is a girl there to whom he has already given fifty dollars for a party. At the same time the first operator shows a large roll of what appears to be money and says he wants to have a good time.

Upon seeing this display of apparent cash, the second bunco operator advises the first one to put his money in a bank before he gets robbed. The first operator demurs, saying that the captain on his ship advised him not to put his money in a "white man's bank" because it was a "one-way deal." A black can deposit money but cannot withdraw it. This statement puts the white victim on the defensive to the extent that he will usually reveal the location of his bank, and further, will attempt to convince the sailor that the information supplied by his captain is false. If the victim is a black, all three may berate the white race; however, the black victim is vulnerable because he wants to prove that he can conduct business the same as a white man.

At this time, the second operator tells the victim that the first operator is ignorant and will lose his money. He further suggests that they, the victim and operator number two, could get some of his money if the victim would be willing to bet operator number one that he could withdraw money from the "white man's bank."

If the victim is a white man, operator number one bets him a considerable amount of cash that he can't withdraw cash from his account. In both instances, whether the victim is a black or white, all three proceed to the bank, where the victim makes a cash withdrawal. After they leave the bank, the second operator tells the sailor (or first bunco operator) that he will take him to see some girls, but that he had better leave his money with the victim temporarily, claiming that the girls are dishonest.

At this time, operator number two sometimes tells his victim to keep all of the money handed over to him by operator number one and that he will meet him later, at which time they will share evenly. If the victim doesn't seem to have enough of a larcenous inclination for this approach, a safekeeping angle is used instead. The victim is told to hold the first operator's money until they return. In either case, the first operator now demands that the victim put his money with the operator's money and hold all of the money together until they return, at which time the victim will receive his winnings, the payoff on his bet that he could withdraw money from a white man's bank. The bunco operator produces a bag and places his roll in the bag, at the same time requiring the victim to do so with his own money as well. The operator then folds the bag and at this time a switch is made, and a bag containing pieces of paper is handed to the victim. Both operators then leave, agreeing to meet the victim later in the day, after they see the girls.

Note how similar this is to the pigeon drop. These bunco games require two operators, both of whom have a rather shrewd knowledge of human behavior. They are smooth enough and sharp enough to play on a victim's greed. In both bunco games, the victim is convinced that he (or she) has a sure thing. In the pigeon drop, the "found" envelope does appear full of money; the Jamaican switch flatters the victim's ego into believing that he could teach the operators a thing or two, and promises him some gain from a bet he knows he will win.

There are a number of variations of the Jamaican switch. If the operators learn that the victim is particularly larcenous and that he is also willing to gamble, he is talked into shooting dice after he gets his money out of the bank. From this point on, the ways in which the bunco operators manage to fleece the victim vary. For example, the second operator may convince the victim that the two of them should arrange to cheat the first operator. On the last roll of the dice, the victim loses but is permitted to write a "bum" check. The first operator goes into a store to cash the check, but comes running out, shouting, "He's calling the police! Run!" All three run, with this one difference. The two bunco operators disappear with the victim's cash.

Another variation of this crime requires a black victim. After he has withdrawn his money, thereby supposedly winning his bet, the sailor mentions that the captain on his ship warned him not to trust any American blacks. The second operator acts indignant and gives his wallet to the first operator and tells him (and the victim) to walk around the block with it while he waits, just to prove his trust. When they return, this act is repeated, except that the victim is now asked to prove his. He turns over his wallet to his two newly found friends, who then walk away with it.

Mexican Charity Switch

The bunco operators in this game can be male or female, and are Spanish-speaking Mexicans, South Americans, or Latin-Americans; they always speak Spanish. The victims are Spanish-speaking Americans, either male or female. To facilitate an explanation of the technique used in this bunco, the first operator will now be identified as #1, and the second as #2.

#1 stops a prospective victim on the street, either male or female, and asks if he (or she) speaks Spanish. If the victim answers affirmatively, #1 engages the victim in conversation in Spanish and asks for help in locating a fictitious person, usually a real-estate agent or an attorney. At this time #2 joins the conversation. #1 then reveals that his father is dying in Mexico (or some other country); that years ago, when his father was in this country, he stole a large sum of money and returned to his native land a rich man. The dying father, attended by a priest, confessed the theft. The priest insisted that before he could give the dying man absolution, he would have to return the money to the United States and distribute it to charity. #1's father told him to locate the fictitious person (the real-estate agent or attorney) and give him the money for distribution. At this time #1 displays what appears to be a large amount of money and states that he has ten thousand dollars (or fifteen thousand dollars, etc.). #1 then asks the victim and also #2 if they will help him, as he wants to return to his father before he dies to tell him his mission was successful.

#1 then tells the victim and #2 that if they can show him that they have money of their own, and will therefore not be tempted by his money, he will give them all the money for them to distribute to charity. #2 leaves the scene and returns later and shows #1 what appears to be a large amount of money. The two bunco operators then ask the victim if he will obtain money to show his good faith, and the victim and one of the operators then proceed to the victim's bank. After the victim obtains his money, the two bunco artists suggest that they all go to the nearest Catholic church and pray. When they get to the church, #1 takes the victim's money and ties it up in a bundle with tight knots. All three go into the church to pray. While they are in the act of praying, handkerchiefs are switched and the victim is given the switched handkerchief. He thinks that he has the handkerchief with all the money tied up in it. #1 then asks #2 to take him to the airport so he can return to his father. The operators leave, telling the victim that #2 will contact him when he returns from the airport. When the victim opens the handkerchief, he finds only folded newspapers.

It may seem to you as though the victim in this bunco is

very naïve. You, however, have been alerted to the fact that this is a confidence game, and you are also aware that the bunco operators are not to be trusted. Remember, however, that shrewd businessmen, and persons who are quite sophisticated and suspicious, are among those who have been duped by operators such as these. Even if you have a knowledge of bunco, you can still become a victim for two reasons: Bunco operators are personable and know how to be extremely charming and ingratiating. Even after they have been arrested, some victims refuse to believe that the bunco operators are what they are, and not what they seem. And, for a second reason, there are so many variations of bunco, with new ones constantly being developed, that no individual is completely immune.

Jamaican Trust Game

Here again (and in all other bunco games to be described) the operators will be identified by number. The Jamaican trust game is characteristically perpetrated by two blacks against a black victim, although other races can be the target for this type of scam. It is usually handled in the following way: #1 approaches a likely victim, and speaking in a strong Jamaican accent, explains that he has just given twenty dollars to a woman for a date, but that she has "run out" on him. Unfamiliar with the laws of this country, he is uncertain what he should do about the incident. The victim explains that it probably would not be good to report the incident to the police, as prostitution is against the law in this country. At about this time, the second bunco operator, #2, joins the scene. He explains to #1 that he can supply him with a beautiful girl at a very reasonable price. #1 agrees to the girl, but expresses some doubt about trusting #2. Somewhat affronted, #2 rallies to his own defense and hands his wallet to #1, suggesting that #1 and the victim walk around the corner with the wallet, just to test the faith of #1. On the way around the block, #1 confides that he has just gotten off ship and has seven hundred dollars on his person. He indicates that he still does not fully trust #1 and asks that his victim keep his money until after the party with the girls. Naturally, there will be a nice, fat reward for the victim's trouble.

Prompted by his own larceny, the victim agrees. Returning after their brief walk, #2 learns of #1's intention to leave his money with the victim and inquires how #1 knows he can trust the victim. #1 defends the victim vigorously, but a cloud of suspicion has been cast, so #2 suggests that the victim give his wallet to #1 and that they (#1 and #2) walk around the corner to prove that the victim has faith and is trustworthy. Taking the victim's wallet, #1 and #2 walk around the corner never to return.

All three of these examples of bunco have one thing in common. They cast doubt on the victim's intentions and require proof of faith. This proof always involves the transfer of money from the victim to the bunco operators. Since proof of faith or trust is a fundamental tenet in many bunco schemes, consider that you will be a victim of bunco should you ever find yourself in a situation in which you are required to demonstrate your good faith, or reliability, or trust, or whatever other virtue the bunco conspirators can dream up.

Paddy Hustle

Young white sevicemen seem extremely vulnerable to this particular type of bunco scheme. Two men, posing as pimps, are characeristically the bunco operators in this hustle. The place where the victim is "taken" is usually a small, down-at-the-heels hotel of the second-floor walk-up variety, equipped with front and rear exits, a community toilet, and a room clerk's desk that is seldom occupied.

In this scam, #1 approaches the victim and offers to get him a girl at a reasonable price. The choice in girls is represented to be wide and varied, ranging from luscious blonde Scandinavian beauties to exotic creamy-complexioned Orientals.

When the victim agrees, he is led to a suitable prearranged

hotel and introduced to operator #2, who is standing behind the clerk's counter and posing as the room clerk. #2 directs #1 and the victim into the community toilet and disappears, ostensibly to see if the girls are ready. Shortly thereafter, the bunco operator reappears and tells the victim there will be a brief wait. At this time the bunco operator tells the victim that although the girls are all or more than represented, they are not trustworthy, and it would be wise for the victim to check his money, watch, and any other valuables with the room clerk until he has finished. To make things appear proper, an envelope is produced in which the victim is to place his ring, watch, and money. Not to be outdone, the victim demands and receives a receipt for his valuables.

Relieved of his possessions, the victim is directed to a room on the second floor. The room may be occupied or not, may be open or locked. In any event, there are no girls and so the victim hurries back to the desk clerk, only to find that the desk clerk and his newly found friend have both vanished.

Because of the embarrassment of the victim, crimes of this kind aren't always reported. That is one reason why crime statistics aren't always as reliable as they may appear to be. Rape is still another kind of crime in which the victim feels ashamed and so does not always complain to the police. If, then, you add a few percentage points to crime statistics, you will probably be much closer to a realistic view of what our crime situation really is. In the case of bunco, it is important that you do not allow yourself to be maneuvered into a position in which you will be expected to hand over your wallet, or a substantial withdrawal from your bank. Many victims are unaware of bunco, or cannot envision themselves in a bunco situation or as being so gullible that they will accept a bunco operation. You can prevent bunco from happening to you by being aware of bunco and alert to its various unfortunate possibilities.

Creepers

This type of bunco scheme is characteristically operated by two prostitutes or a prostitute and an accomplice. The prostitute picks up her "mark" (victim) in a bar or on the street, and accompanies him to a prearranged location where the accomplice is waiting. The location is a dark, suitably equipped room in which to turn a "trick" (engage in an act of prostitution). After the couple disrobes and while they are engaged in the sex act, the accomplice creeps into the room from a place of concealment, and removes valuables from the victim's clothing, which has been placed on some convenient chair.

When getting dressed, the victim will discover his loss soon enough, but it is difficult for him to point the finger of blame at the prostitute, for she has been in his company all the time. Even if he persists he will seldom be successful, for the lady is on her home grounds and surrounded by her friends, accomplices, and pimps who are ready to come to her aid. Outnumbered, outshouted, and outtalked, the victim soon realizes he is no physical match for such a group. Again, this type of crime is often unreported. And if reported, all that may happen is that the prostitute will be held overnight, will pay a fine in the morning, and will be back in business the same day, or night. The proceeds from the victim may be more than enough to pay all costs.

The Badger Game

Men seeking sex are vulnerable to all sorts of games, such as the one just described. Still another, known as the badger game, is usually accomplished by a prostitute and a male friend, and follows a definite pattern.

As a start the lady, often quite attractive, allows herself to be picked up by the mark. She further allows him to make friendly advances and at the proper time, seemingly overcome by his maleness, good looks, and wit, permits him to take her to her private apartment. At the peak of the evening's entertainment, the lady's "husband" returns unexpectedly and is outraged. The husband, though, isn't so overcome that he forgets his camera, conveniently loaded, properly focused, and prepared to take repeated shots of the naked couple.

The victim is now ripe for extortion. His name, address, and business are known to the woman, who has been careful to obtain this information prior to the appearance of her husband. If not, or if the mark has insisted on retaining his anonymity, it is no great effort for the husband to reach for the victim's wallet and extract his business card, and possibly some cash as well.

That cash isn't the end of it, for now the victim is at the losing end of an extortion scheme. Depending on their wealth, victims of such schemes will often pay and pay, rather than run the risk of exposure.

There are many variations of the badger game. A seductive young prostitute, for example, may select one of her higher-priced clientele as the mark. She takes her patron to a particular motel that is decorated in the most fashionable manner and noted for its discreetness. After engaging in sex with the prostitute, the businessman returns to his everyday existence.

A day or two later he receives a telephone call from the manager of the motel, who explains that either Mr. Businessman or his "wife" must have left a cigarette burning in their room, as the motel had a serious fire that destroyed considerable, expensive furnishings in Mr. Businessman's suite. The manager further explains that the insurance-company representative requested him to call to see if a lawsuit could be avoided.

Obviously, the businessman might be inclined to pay for the damages. If he checks the premises, he will find evidence of the fire that will substantiate a lawsuit. Because Mr. Businessman's wife might be upset by the circumstances, situations of this type are often settled out of court.

Marriage Bunco

Marriage bunco is one of the saddest of all the schemes used for separating people from their money and valuable possessions, for it takes advantage of their loneliness and their desire to build a personal relationship. There are many people who are alone, widows who have been accustomed to a long-term male-female relationship, and young women who seem unable to meet the right man. Such persons often advertise in local newspapers for friends, readily engage in correspondence with strangers, are relatively easy pickups, join lonely-hearts clubs, or attend dances for the sole purpose of meeting someone. They are all ready, and easy, prey for the marriage-bunco operator. Although operators of such schemes can be male or female, this particular type of bunco seems to attract a larger number of men. The male operator is characteristically well-dressed, manages to convey an impression of wealth, is an easy and good conversationalist, knows how to put women at their ease; is sympathetic, kind, courteous, gentle, considerate. The victim, on the other hand, has often had little experience with men, and, as in the case with many widows, may have led a relatively sheltered life. Quite often the woman is a person of modest means, generally with just a few thousand dollars set aside for immediate personal or old-age security.

After initial introductions, and careful interrogation and analysis, the con man chooses his mark. He then sets off on a whirlwind courtship, flattering the woman and giving her the undivided attention she yearns for and that she often believes she is entitled to. At some point, when the bunco operator feels that his prospect has become adequately "softened," he proposes marriage and is nearly always accepted immediately, without hesitation, without investigation. His own description of himself, of his business, and of his life, are accepted without challenge. Quite often the woman wonders at her tremendous good fortune.

Shortly after they become engaged, the victim is told that although she is loved the actual wedding will have to be postponed until the bunco artist's funds are released from escrow in another city. He explains that he has recently sold his business, and that all his assets will be tied up for about six months pending transfer of title to the new owner. The bunco operator then suggests that the marriage can take place immediately, however, if she will lend him a substantial sum. The bunco operator has long since learned of his fiancée's cash resources and is able to indicate just what the required amount will be.

The woman generally withdraws her entire savings and gives it to the bunco operator without hesitation. After all, their money will all be in the family once the marriage ceremony is performed. A slick con man can often maneuver his victim into a position in which she proposes the loan, while he demurs and appears to resist but finally capitulates to her demands that he take the money. The more reluctant he appears, the more she insists. Finally, he accepts the cash, and is then never seen again.

There are many variations that bunco operators use in marriage bunco. Some are equipped with fancy gilt-edged stock certificates, or deeds to real estate, or bundles of documents, all of which tend to convey an impression of wealth; not cash, but wealth that can be turned into cash at some future date. The basic bunco remains the same, though—the separation of money from the victim under the promise or inducement of marriage. Marriage-bunco operators seldom marry their victims, since most of them don't want to become involved with bigamy laws in the event they are apprehended. One notorious Los Angeles operator, however, married twenty-six women and successfully separated them from their savings before he was caught.

The Moneymaking Machine

It would seem that only someone who was naïve or stupid would accept or believe in a bunco scheme and indeed, some of the schemes are crude. But some buncos are extremely sophisticated and involve considerable preparation and planning. Many otherwise intelligent people have purchased stock in gold mines that did not exist, in oil wells that were never drilled, in real estate located completely under water, in apartment houses that would never be constructed. Quite often referred to as investments, or more blatantly as a once-in-a-lifetime chance to get rich, or an opportunity to "be your own boss," they have worked successfully against all types of people. No individual can claim immunity against a bunco scheme. If the bunk appeals to our vanity, desire to be financially independent, wish to stop working, or whatever the need or want may be, somewhere there is a bunco artist ready to take advantage. The bunco operator's problem isn't developing a scheme—that he can do. His big problem is making contact with suitable victims.

The moneymaking machine is another bunco scheme, and while it seems impossible that anyone in his right mind would fall for it, yet it is used regularly and successfully. As a general rule, this form of bunco is worked by a person of foreign extraction against victims of similar heritage. The victim doesn't just happen, but is selected. Once that is done, the con man begins a campaign to impress the victim, including lavish entertainment and an apparent never-ending supply of new bills. Ultimately, the victim notices that the bills never seem to be old or used and finally asks about it. Ultimately, after considerable urging, the con man reveals the source of his money: a moneymaking machine. The victim is skeptical at first but the bunco operator demonstrates the machine by opening two compartments; into one he puts a crisp new twenty-dollar bill, and into the other he has the victim put a piece of blank white bond paper. Cautioning the victim not to stand too near the machine, the con man begins to operate the dials and levers, increasing the humming sound from within the machine. While handling the impressive array of levers and dials, the con man pushes a hidden lever that causes a secret compartment to replace the one containing the bond paper. After an appropriate time, some sort of signal sounds, such as a bell. The con man opens both compartments; from one he removes the original twenty-dollar bill and from the other another twenty-dollar bill, which has apparently just been printed.

The victim is now encouraged to take this new bill to a bank and to verify it for authenticity. This, after all, is the real proof. The victim agrees and, the moment he learns that the bill is genuine, is hooked.

From this point on, there are various methods that can be used to induce the victim to part with his money. One way is to let him buy the machine. The con man can explain that he has had the machine for a long time and is willing to share his good fortune. Another technique is to explain that the machine gradually deteriorates each of the original bills used, and to make a run of new money, needs a large supply of new bills to speed the moneymaking process. The victim rushes to his bank, withdraws all his savings in new bills, and gives them to the con man, who then agrees to have a duplicate set ready in a few hours. Of course, when the victim returns, both his recent friend and his machine are gone.

Short-Change Artists

Most people don't like to do arithmetic, and they especially do not like it if it involves any mental effort. And so, it is easy to get short-changed in any retail establishment where the cashier is interested in making a few extra dollars. The short-change tehnique is usually practiced on transient trade, and works best when there is a long line of customers waiting at the cash register. Some people do not even bother to count their change, while others may suspect they haven't received the correct change but are too embarrassed to do anything about it, particularly if they are in a strange area.

There also are, of course, short-change artists who are customers. One example is the con man who makes a 25¢ purchase, but almost immediately changes his mind and increases it to 50¢. He then pays with a ten-dollar bill and gets $9.50 in change. The bunco operator then states he made a mistake and did not want so much change. He produces and retains possession of five one-dollar bills and a five-dollar bill and asks for a ten-dollar bill in exchange. The victim gives the con artist a ten-dollar bill, but does not take possession of the con man's money. The latter slaps the five ones, the five-, and the ten-dollar bill together and asks for a twenty-dollar bill in exchange. The victim gives the con man a twenty-dollar bill and gets the miscellaneous twenty dollars in exchange.

In retrospect, the involved underlying theft might seem quite apparent, but consider that the exchanges in money take place quite rapidly, accompanied by a distracting chatter from the con man. The con man knows precisely what he is doing; the victim is confused and quickly loses track of who gave what to whom.

Bunco Crimes Involving Police Impersonations

There are many crimes committed by individuals who use police impersonation as part of their MO's (*modus operandi*). These scams often take the form of a shakedown racket in which victims are subject to phony arrests by bogus officers. The incident giving rise to the phony arrest is usually set up by the phony cops to pave the way for acceptance of cash bail or the way for solicitation of a phony bribe.

Like other criminals, suspects engaged in police impersonation become specialists in their field and play a convincing policeman role. Most victims, when interviewed, remain convinced they were dealing with real policemen. On the West Coast, the bribery or bail-posting schemes are called "shakes" by both the perpetrator and the police. At the present time, there are several phony-arrest routine variations:

1. The Abortion Shake

The abortion shake can be set up in one of two ways. One such operation is set up and controlled in the same manner used by actual detectives. A female operator, posing as the typical unwed, pregnant female, obtains an appointment for an illegal abortion. The abortionist, naturally, is arrested just prior to the illegal operation. Thus, the stage is set for extortion or bribery. In continuance of the phony arrest scam, the mark is allowed to make cash bail, without going through elaborate booking procedures.

2. The Bookmaker Shake

Phony-cop arrest schemes can be adapted to any type of criminal situation. Things go smoothest when the victim is caught in the commission of an actual crime, or when they think they have done so.

In states where bookmaking is a crime, bookmakers are sometimes ready victims for a phony bribe shakedown for purported police protection. Sooner or later, the hoax is discovered, so such shakedowns are generally temporary, and are usually most successful against novice bookmakers.

In areas where certain activities, such as prostitution, abortion, shooting dice, smoking marijuana, or betting parlors are illegal, since the victims are law violators, they are susceptible to shakedown artists because they are not in a position to call for police protection.

3. The Badger Game Shake

Another type of shake is a variation of the badger game with the familiar irate husband and movie camera being replaced by police impersonators. With a prearranged stage, a pair of bogus vice officers enter the dimly lighted boudoir and arrest the mark, probably in some stage of undress. The normal victim usually has a wife and family, a good job or business, and a healthy fear of publicity, all of which curb his enthusiasm for tangling with the "authorities." If he is lucky, it may cost him no more than the total contents of his wallet. If not, he may be susceptible to continued blackmail.

4. The Fruit Shake

The fruit shake is a phony cop–homosexual shakedown racket. In the past, a phony cop would locate a homosexual hangout, such as a bar or public toilet used by homosexuals. With some small encouragement, the homosexual would make advances and then be arrested by the phony cop, who simply showed his badge and possibly an impressive card stamped "Police Department" and carrying his photo. The homosexual and the phony detective would then start walking toward the police station, but would be joined by a second phony detective. This second bogus detective would explain that they had an urgent call to make and suggest that the victim make bail right there. The two detectives then would settle for as much money as they could squeeze out of the homosexual. The "arrested" person quite naturally assumed that he has just bribed a pair of police officers who, like all police officers, are dishonest anyway.

In recent years, however, homosexuals have been further victimized by a decoy called the lugger who locates victims. The decoy suggests a place that is clandestine and lugs the victim past a pair of "shakemen" or bogus police officers enroute to his quiet place. Wherever the victim is taken, he is allowed to put himself in a compromising position, and it is at that time the shakemen appear and arrest both parties. The decoy pleads for his freedom, but to no avail, and he is taken away, apparently to jail since he is an old offender and well-known to the officers.

The victim, on the other hand, is told he is different from the general run of people found involved in this type of activity, and he is sternly warned never to be seen in the area again. A good shakeman normally can get considerable information about family, friends, background, job, and financial status from the victim, who panics and blurts out answers to any questions asked him. Subtle pressures are brought to bear and the victim is certain that if he is arrested every newspaper in his neighborhood will print the story, exposing his sexual deviation to the world and ruining him.

One of the policemen appears to be kind and understanding and the victim is released and immediately rushes off, relieved at his unexpected good fortune. Three or four days later, the officers appear at the victim's home or his place of employment, explaining that the other person who was arrested has consulted an attorney, who now demands to know why both persons weren't arrested. At this time, one of the phony policemen explains that an arrest warrant has been issued, but in another name, and the payment for his kindness is that he is now in trouble.

Again, the victim panics, but he is offered a way out by the policemen, who agree to let him post bail under the name of the person on the arrest warrant. The policemen explain that there would then be no need for fingerprinting, photographs, or for booking the victim in the local police station. The victim usually drives to his bank with the phony officers and makes bail right on the spot.

In the words of one shakeman, "You start high with the bail amount because you can always come down, but there is just no way to go up. Scores of five thousand dollars are common and during part of one year there were reported individual losses of twenty, fifteen, and ten thousand dollars in about a dozen fruit shakes that were ultimately brought to the attention of a police department.

5. The Till Tap

Till taps aren't common, but they do illustrate the ingenuity used by some con artists. Here is the way a till tap works against a liquor store, although any other kind of store can be victimized. One of the con men enters the store and at that moment the clerk receives a phone call asking to speak to Detective ———. The clerk asks his customer if he is Detective ———. The phony detective admits that he is and answers the phone, apparently having a conversation with his local precinct regarding a possible robbery. The detective then advises the clerk that he has just been informed that the store is about to be held up and that a stakeout is necessary. The detective advises the clerk to take the money out of the cash register and to put it in a paper bag and to put the bag in a designated spot at the rear of the store. The detective then asks the clerk to lend him his clerk's apron or store jacket, so that he can pretend to be the clerk. He advises the clerk that for his own safety it would be best if he left for a short time; there might be a shootout. The clerk leaves, and upon returning finds that both the detective and the paper bag with the cash receipts are gone.

Pickpockets and Purse Picks

Statistics indicate that one out of every twelve urbanites will be a pickpocket victim, and that the majority will be elderly men and women.

A pickpocket may work alone or in groups of two or three. The professional pickpocket is one of the highest types of mechanical criminals. He is an expert in human nature and accomplished in every trick of distraction and knowledge of human reflexes. By using psychology and planned physical reaction, he skillfully maneuvers a victim into a position in which his wallet can be easily removed.

Pickpockets operate in many different ways. The basic theory is: "You can't steal a man's money if he has his mind on it." The timing of the theft is planned on the principle of misdirection. Thus, when the victim directs his interests to activities at sporting events, or if he (or she) is getting on a bus or train, or buying food or clothing, his attention is concentrated on a specific activity rather than on awareness of his general environment. And because the victim is concentrating on some other activity, he becomes unaware of what the pickpocket is doing. It is literally impossible to concentrate fully on your wallet or pocketbook. Taking an upward step into a bus, for example, means you must be highly conscious of the movement of your feet, and whether you realize it or not, this simple physical act does require concentration, even though you may not be mentally aware of what you are doing. You may be daydreaming or thinking of something else while you step upward into the bus, yet part of you directs your mental activities, the other part the physical.

But even assuming you have a high level of wallet or pocket-book awareness, there are many ways in which the victim can be distracted. He may be accidentally burned by a cigarette. The pickpocket, in a restaurant, may accidentally spill a glass of water on him. There are amorous women pickpockets who put their arms around a victim, rub against him, and at the same time pick his pocket. The pickpocket may jostle or bump against the victim, and may do so strongly and so obviously deliberately that the first reaction of the victim is one of resentment. It does not matter. The victim has been distracted.

A pickpocket has a limited time in which to operate. He often cannot distract you more than once without arousing your suspicions. Keep your wallet where the pickpocket cannot reach it, and make it difficult for him to remove. In some instances pickpockets will work in groups of three. They crowd the victim, and with two of them pushing and jostling, the third does his work. Again, if your wallet isn't readily available, as it would be in a hip pocket, they will move along to a more likely prospect.

How to Protect Yourself Against Pickpockets

1. Always try to be aware of your money or your purse while shopping, in crowds, in elevators, buses, and public places.

2. If you are jostled on a bus in a crowd, or someone stumbles into you, make sure immediately that your wallet and/or money are intact.

3. Don't display large sums of money in public.

4. Don't carry your wallet in your hip pocket in crowds, buses, etc. It is the easiest pocket to pick, even if you have your coat buttoned. When you buy a wallet, select the long, thin kind that will hold dollar bills flat, without folding them. A bulging breast pocket is an out-and-out invitation to a pickpocket.

5. Don't put your handbook down on a counter, on the floor, or in a shopping cart. If your put your pocketbook down on a luncheon counter, for example, it can disappear in the single

moment you turn your head away. A pickpocket or a handbook thief can be incredibly fast.

6. Remember not to carry, suspended over your arm, a clasptype handbag that, when opened, will open away from your body.

7. When carrying open-type purses or basket types, don't have a wallet or money visible.

8. Don't carry loose bills—from dollar bills to those of higher denominations—or purses, or wallets in a coat or sweater pocket when shopping.

9. When carrying an armload of packages, keep your purse between your body and the packages.

10. When a stranger starts a conversation with you, stay aware of your wallet and your money. This is a very common diversionary gambit.

11. If you are approached by strangers who start conversations as to aches and pains, rheumatism, or other illness and proceed to touch you, or they tell you they are medical people, or are able to heal you by touch—watch out! They are touching your money as well.

12. Beware of approaches by individuals who claim to be from the general hospital or from Social Security and want to check you physically for a possible hike in pension. The only thing they want to hike is their bunco income.

13. Beware of kindly individuals who assist you in crossing the street, or who want to help you onto a bus, or want to help you adjust your packages.

14. A common ploy used by female pickpockets is to drop a compact, a book, a bag and wait for you, a gentleman at all times, to pick it up for her. She may be a woman pickpocket inviting you to bend over to give her a chance at your wallet as you do.

The average pickpocket usually uses an object, such as a newspaper or a coat over the arm, to hide his actions or to dispose of your wallet, when taken.

Gypsies

Gypsies, with no formal education other than the practical psychology learned in everyday life, swindle most people who come to them for help as easily as taking candy from a baby. Their victims are most often elderly people.

Fortunetelling is one of the most common techniques for providing the Gypsy with a supply of victims for major bunco. The Gypsy gets victims by advertising in local newspapers, by distributing circulars from door to door, or by renting a store front and soliciting transient trade.

First, the victim has his fortune told for a modest fee ranging from about two to ten dollars. By skillful interrogation the Gypsy is able to learn about the victim's problems and financial standing. Next, the Gypsy assures the victim of the power of prayer, offering to pray and to burn candles for a price, depending on how large a candle the victim wishes burned. Victims are told that there are evil spirits within their bodies which cause their problems and these evil spirits are caused by money, "the root of all evil."

To confirm her supernatural prowess, the Gypsy may demonstrate by having the victim bring in a raw egg, and by sleight of hand, may substitute an egg having a black mass in it. After the victim is convinced that his body also contains evil spirits, and that his money is the cause, the rest is easy. The victim is told to bring in a large amount, the larger the bills the better. The Gypsy takes the money and tells the victim that it will be flushed down a toilet, thrown in the ocean, or buried in a cemetery. Sometimes they will ask the victim to throw the money in the ocean after placing the money in a cloth bag and sewing the ends. While the victim's attention is distracted, the bag is switched.

Gypsies also engage in faith healing. They are accomplished pickpockets. Working as a team, they will approach a victim and ask for information. The victims are questioned about their health and an offer to pray for them is made. While praying, the Gypsies run their hands over the victim's body and at the same time pick his pockets. Young girls will approach elderly men and rub their bodies to excite them. While the victim is distracted, his pocket is being picked.

Other Gypsy crimes involve gem repair, body and fender repair, plating, roof and driveway coating, and insurance frauds.

The Williamsons

The Williamsons are a Gypsy-type clan of door-to-door solicitors who have been swindling the public for more than fifty years. Presently, they are primarily engaged in oiling roofs and driveways with a substandard grade of oil diluted with inflammable solvent or water. The method used is nearly always the same. The salesman approaches the home owner with a story that he has just enough oil left over from a commercial job and will repair a roof for under a hundred dollars. A useless ten- to twenty-year guarantee against leaks is supplied verbally and the roof is "repaired" in about twenty minutes. Sometimes they quote no price and demand five hundred dollars or more from elderly victims, and by intimidation, frighten them into paying.

The Williamsons have been called the "terrible Williamsons" and the "Williamson-McMillan Gang." The exact number in the group is unknown, but estimates run from three hundred to five hundred. They are a clannish group that marry only within the group, mingling with outsiders only to relieve them of their money. The names of individuals in the group are Williamson, McMillan, Daly, Stewart, Carrol, Johnson, Gregg, Halliday, and McDonald. They invariably have a Scottish accent and drive immaculately kept model pickup trucks with new spray equipment. They are reported to have amassed vast real-estate holdings from their profits in the roof-oiling business.

In bunco, as in business, success attracts competitors. Not only the Williamsons, but other bunco artists are engaged in door-to-door selling of house repairs. They will try to sell you outdoor siding, patios, cement work, brick work, painting. They are often high-pressure types whose interest is to get you to sign a contract and make a down payment. The contract may bind you to some very shoddy work at an exorbitant price. To avoid such schemes, use contractors who have offices in your area and whom you can visit if you want. If you have the slightest doubt, call, or write to the Better Business Bureau in your area.

Magazine Solicitors

Door-to-door magazine solicitors are often con men, just as unscrupulous as the man who sidles up to you in the street and asks if you are interested in buying a "hot" watch or ring. Magazine salesmen are often women, but there is no sexual restriction.

The magazine bunco may work alone or together with another solicitor. The usual pitch is that he is engaged in a popularity contest that will enable him to win a scholarship for college or a cash award to enable him to go into business. Rarely will the solicitor admit he is selling magazines, even under the most direct questioning, until he has gained admittance to your house. Once inside, the solicitor expertly scrutinizes you and your home for things that can be used as a basis for his sales pitch. If he spots a religious symbol, he will automatically be of your religion or studying for the ministry, and will try to sell you religious magazines. If he spots law books, he will be studying to be a lawyer. In any event, he will try to find some common ground of conversation that he can use for his sales pitch.

Whatever story the bunco operator may give, his sole purpose is to induce you to buy a magazine subscription. Once you are committed to a purchase, you are then encouraged to pay in cash. Naturally, if you don't have the cash, a check is acceptable, but the salesman will try to induce you to leave the "pay to the order of" section blank, stating that the company name will be stamped in later. Once out of your home, the solicitor will write in the word "cash" or his name in this portion, and will immediately cash it at a local store where you are known, or at your bank.

Here is how you can protect yourself from these types:

1. Don't permit any outside door-to-door salesman to enter your home under any circumstances.

2. Never buy on impulse. The bunco artist will try to pressure you with magazines at tremendous savings, or merchandise, or labor services. You will be told it is the "last one," or that you are the only one to have been selected for this bargain, or that they will make their profit through your recommendations, or that this is positively the last day of this sale. Just tell the solicitor to leave his card, or to write his name and address, and you will check him out.

3. If you do permit the con man inside your home, do not leave him alone for a moment. Their usual ploy is to wait in the living room, pretend they are thirsty, and ask for a drink of water. In the short time you will be away, things of value will disappear.

4. If you must buy, do not pay in cash, and never give an incompletely filled check.

5. Never accept verbal promises. Take written statements only.

6. Never, never sign anything. If you are pressured to sign, indicate firmly that you must first consult your attorney.

7. If you are seriously interested in getting a bargain, no matter what the bargain may be, contact the publisher, or the manufacturer, or the distributor directly. They are as close to you as your telephone.

The Religious Bunco

"Your doorstep is our pulpit!"

It may never occur to you to question a person dressed in clerical garb, and yet he may just be a con man in disguise. Like all con men, the unscrupulous religious solicitor presents a picture in keeping with the impression he wants you to have. His clothing may vary from a Salvation-Army-type hat to a complete clerical outfit. His props usually include religious literature and he may even have a Bible in his hand.

When you answer your doorbell, the con man explains his noble purpose and asks you to make a donation for the purchase of Bibles for distribution to the poor. On some occasions, the con operator will ask for admittance to your home to pray for your salvation (and for your generosity). After this conditioning process, he will ask you to donate whatever your conscience dictates for "God's work."

But take a look at how each dollar collected is divided: Sixty cents will go to the solicitor who met you at your door as his wages; ten cents to a crew manager who transports and supervises a crew of solicitors who will cover your neighborhood like a swarm of locusts; twenty-five cents are earmarked for business overhead expense, which includes rent for the so-called church, generally a converted store with a few benches and perhaps a podium complete with a pulpit, and wages for the persons providing the corporate name. Only the remainder, if there is a remainder, will actually be used for the purchase of Bibles for the poor.

Although this operation is unethical, it is not illegal. Most of these organizations are incorporated as nonprofit religious corporations; they are legally classified as churches and are exempt from taxation. They are permitted to solicit donations for their church.

How can you protect yourself and still not turn away those who are entitled to your consideration? The simplest method is not to give money to questionable organizations at your door under any circumstances. If an organization is legitimate, the solicitor should not mind identifying himself and supplying his local business address. When in doubt, telephone your local enforcement agency and ask about the organization.

Your Self-Protection

Bunco operators can take advantage of you in many, many ways. They are shrewd judges of human nature and can spot your particular weakness in a matter of seconds. To protect yourself:

- Never sign anything.
- Always delay. Ask them to come back some other time.
- Advise the door-to-door operator that you want to check with your husband (or your wife), or to give you the phone number of a satisfied neighbor, or that you want to talk to your lawyer.
- Keep in mind that nobody in this wide, wide world has the slightest interest in making you rich, or famous, or beautiful, or strong, or well-educated, unless you supply them with a very good financial reason for doing so.
- Stay away from get-rich-quick schemes.
- Don't buy merchandise that is offered to you as "hot."
- An easy way to check on a door-to-door salesman is to learn if the company he claims to represent is in the Yellow Pages of the phone book, but remember that even some fly-by-night outfits manage to get themselves listed.
- Don't be flattered if a solicitor comes to your door and addresses you by name. He may have obtained this from the nameplate on your door or he may have asked a neighbor.
- Don't fall for schemes in which you are asked to buy some product for a very low price, just for advertising purposes.
- Don't agree to schemes in which your home will be used as a sales center to which all your neighbors will be invited, and for which you will receive some kind of product without charge.
- Don't buy raffles, so-called chances, or tickets from strangers who appear at your door. Tickets for benefits are usually for the sole benefit of the con man.
- Never invite a door-to-door salesman into your home. Don't allow him to work his way in. A common ploy is for the salesman to ask for a drink of water.
- Don't be taken in by the con man's apparel. He may appear in religious garb, may seem to be blind and guided by a seeing-eye dog, or may appear to be injured or wounded in some way. Some bunco operators have stories that would melt the heart of a stone Indian.
- Don't be taken in by the youth or apparent innocence of

the solicitor. Some con men use very young girls or very young boys as a front. These young people may not be aware of what they are doing, but they are being manipulated.

· At one time a man's home was his castle. Today it must be his fortress. The person out there on your steps may look helpless, frightened, weary, and as if he were just trying to make an honest dollar. Given the opportunity, he may deprive you of your money and possibly your life as well.

All of this may sound harsh and perhaps it is. It is also possible that you may turn away worthy people, people who may deserve your help and consideration. Remember, though, that there are many organizations devoted to helping such people, and if you do want to help, you can do no better than to make your contribution directly. If someone does ask you for help, you can do so by referring them to an established organization.

· Don't be fooled by badges, identity cards, or letters from companies. All of these can be faked or forged, and often are.

· Many bunco door-to-door operators never sell anything. You will be asked to help someone who is working his way through college, or to contribute to some worthy cause. Quite often the opening ploy of the con man is to ask you some questions, to get you to talk to him. If you refuse to "play the game," or if you make it quite clear that you don't intend to buy or to donate, he may make an attempt to make you feel quilty, or contemptible. Don't let it bother you. It's better to feel guilty than to feel like a sucker.

The Lemon Game

Some bunco operators are highly expert in some form of gambling or may be poolroom sharks. The card con man may fumble the deck, ask questions that reveal ignorance of the fundamentals of a particular card game, and often show a large roll of bills; he will brag about his ability at cards while making it quite obvious he is a complete amateur. In short, what he is doing, and doing quite skillfully, is putting himself in a position to be taken. This has a double appeal for the mark. First, the mark may be motivated by some slight stirring of larceny at the sight of all the money being displayed. And, second, the con man's attitude is so obnoxious that the potential victim is determined to teach him a lesson. Now, this may be rationalization since greed is probably the main factor pushing the mark into suggesting a game of cards.

Another type of confidence game known as the lemon game involves the use of a pool table. While this type of confidence game isn't too widespread, there are enough amateurs who play a fair game of pool and possibly overestimate their own abilities to make this type of con game possible.

The "lemon man" will have all the main characteristics of a successful bunco operator. He will have a glib tongue and a sharp mind, both essential for someone who lives by his wits. He is usually a highly extroverted person, is congenial, and has the ability to meet people and make friends quite easily. He is a superb actor and not only understands human psychology but is a master at its application. Equally important, he is an expert at playing pool, and is far more competent at it than most amateurs.

The lemon man is usually found in a poolroom, but unlike amateur players, shoots a very restrained game of pool, and does not allow his skill to manifest itself. If anything, viewers will come to the conclusion that he is quite below average, a little better than a raw beginner. More recently the lemon man has shifted his base of operations to the bar that offers a pool table for the amusement of its patrons. The reason for this is that a mark with several drinks in him is much more susceptible to being goaded into accepting the challenge of a game.

In a typical operation, the con man strikes up an acquaintance with the victim and suggests a game of pool, just to pass the time or just for fun, or for some other seemingly harmless reason. To make the game interesting, he then suggests they play for the cost of the game. This is just the opening gambit, though, for the con man proceeds to lose each game. He is quite capable of demonstrating his lack of skill and does so very convincingly. After several games, during which he seems to become more upset after losing successively, he suggests to the victim that they double the bet to give the con man an opportunity to recoup his losses.

Here is where the skill of the lemon man becomes important. He always manages to win, now, by extremely small margins, apparently doing so only by a fluke, while convincing the mark that each game has been won by pure chance. The victim, of course, has long since been convinced he is the superior player and his ego readily regards his growing losses as accidental.

Meanwhile, the bets are increased in size and the victim falls more and more in debt to his "lucky" opponent. By this time, it is now the victim who suggests doubling the bets so he can get even. However, the bunco operator carefully continues to win, allowing the victim to win occasionally to maintain his confidence. If worked properly, the lemon-game operator soon owns the entire contents of his victim's wallet.

In a bunco of this kind, there is very little law authorities can do. When the victim cooperates with the con man, as in the lemon game, there is little the police can do to protect the individual against the consequences of his own actions. The law cannot protect people against their own stupidity.

Phony-Bank-Examiner Shake

Elderly women are often the favorite targets of con men and women for several reasons. Such women are generally unsophisticated and have usually been protected for most of their lives, first by a father and then by a husband. Since the male mortality rate is much higher than that of the female, such women are usually widows. In many cases they live on a fixed income such as Social Security or Social Security combined with a small pension, meanwhile keeping their lifetime savings in a bank as a bulwark. They are often lonely and equally often welcome the attention of people.

The phony-bank-examiner game, like the pigeon drop, is generally employed against women of this type. The most frequent sites of these operations are residential areas, especially apartment-house districts, near shopping and small business centers that have local banks.

Confidence men using the phony-bank-examiner scheme work in two- or three-man teams, are usually successful, and often manage to avoid arrest by selecting their victims carefully and proceeding with great caution throughout the entire transaction. They do not hesitate to modify their plan of operation as they go along to assure success and minimize detection. As an example, if the victim contacts anyone other than those she is instructed to meet, the con men will stop their activities and look for a different prospect.

This bunco begins with a telephone call to the victim. The caller identifies himself as a bank official, assuming a role such as an examiner, or an auditor. His first move is to throw the victim off emotional balance. He does this quite easily by telling the victim that the bank has been experiencing some losses in its accounts, including hers. Completely distraught at the prospect of losing her nest egg, the victim is now given an opportunity not only to recoup her purported losses, but to make a substantial profit as well.

The con man asks the help of the victim in catching the thief and offers a reward of cash or bonds as an inducement. She is also told that the bank examiners are not yet aware that money has disappeared from her account, and that if she makes a substantial withdrawal before they find out, the loss will be the bank's, not hers. If the victim agrees, the con man with some adroit questioning determines the maximum amount the woman has in the bank, and the name of the bank. He then advises her to withdraw a specified amount, not enough to close out the account, but with just a few dollars remaining in it.

The victim is cautioned not to discuss this investigation with anyone, particularly with bank officials, so as not to alarm the thief who has been pilfering her account, and so as to make her eligible for the reward. She is told that if the thief should disappear, she will lose the money in her account as well as the reward. She is also told to get the money in cash and not to handle the money so as not to destroy the suspect's fingerprints.

Originally, the victim was instructed to return to her home, where a detective or bank investigator or official examiner would retrieve the money and return it to her account at the bank. At that time she would also receive her reward for her cooperation. In a subsequent modification of this bunco, the victim is told that just after she leaves the bank an official will approach her and identify himself with a code word or number. The victim would then be required to turn the money over to this person.

There is one unusual aspect to this particular bunco, and it is one reason why the operators are so seldom apprehended. Note that the victim never sees the con men. The only time she does is when she turns the money over to the official meeting her in the street. This meeting is so brief and the victim so excited, not only about assuring the safety of her funds, but also about the substantial reward promised to her, that she is invariably unable to give any description of the person to whom she gives her money.

Again, this bunco seems to violate common sense and ordinary prudence and it would seem that the female victims should know better. Keep in mind though, that somewhere there is a bunco operator scheming against your funds, and that you, in turn, may be as ready a victim. There is a little larceny in nearly all of us and con men know it. They can tailor any scheme, make it as naïve or as sophisticated as you might imagine, with full knowledge of the psychology and predictable human behavior of their victims.

Gold-Sale Bunco

Gold has always had a fascinating attraction and for some an almost mystical appeal. Probably one of the earliest of the bunco schemes consisted of painting bricks a gold color and then finding a suitable victim. In some instances the victims were more plentiful than the bricks. It is absolutely amazing what the human mind will believe when it wants to believe. A large part of the success of the bunco operator stems from the fact that the victim is so capable of self-delusion. He wants to believe in Santa Claus. He wants to believe he is deserving of immediate wealth, of reward, and in his mind he sees nothing illogical in his acquiring the so-called easy buck. If this yearning for quick money were not such a part of our mental makeup, there would be no bunco schemes or bunco operators.

Gold-sale bunco schemes range all the way from the crude yellow-painted brick to shares of stock in nonexistent gold mines. A common bunco scheme in the midwest of the nineteenth century was to "salt" a mine with bits of gold, have an invited visitor "find" them, and then invite him to share in the phenomenal luck of this strike by buying shares in the mine.

There have been, and there still are, and there possibly always will be, bunco gold schemes of varying degrees of sophistication. People still buy shares in mines they have never seen and have never investigated, simply on the word of a glib con man and the allure of a colorful, impressive, well-printed prospectus. In one recent bunco, eight cans, each holding three gallons, were deposited with an armored car company. Each of the cans was supposed to contain a liquid gold concentrate having a value of about a half-million dollars. The owners of the concentrate then tried to establish a line of unlimited credit with a local bank purely on the basis of this collateral. In one instance, someone had the common sense to insist that the gold concentrate be tested. Of course, it was found to be worthless. But what is even more interesting is that this scheme was tried and did succeed. The bunco amount was close to a million dollars. This scheme, which apparently should not fool even a schoolboy, fooled some bank executives and will be tried again and will succeed again.

The basic requirement for a gold-bunco scheme is a good front man, a convincing and glib talker, one who can discuss the subject of gold with force and intelligence. The second con man involved in the swindle sometimes acts as the appraiser, and he too will talk and behave convincingly as an expert. All that is needed is a victim—and there are plenty of those— and some sort of scheme. The scheme need not be elaborate or even exceptionally well-planned.

A successful swindle requires that the victim pay his money without ever seeing what he buys. He may have been induced to do this through conversations, falsified letters of credit, falsified certificates of deposit, falsified assay reports, stupidity or greed, or a combination of any of these.

Not only is this bunco suitable for the sale of gold, but it is regularly done today with real estate. Newspapers carry advertising appealing to a basic human instinct: a home out in the woods, or by the sea, or up in the mountains, anywhere away from it all where a man can be master of everything he surveys, far from the grubbiness and pettiness of the daily struggle for existence. The sale of desert land, for example, is often done by elaborately printed color brochures showing swimming pools, roads, trees, shrubbery, mountains in the distance, plus promises of a pure environment. The victims may be invited to a free dinner where they are shown slides of what is purported to be the continued development of the property. Through flattery, pressure, and every other trick known by con men, the victim is persuaded to pay and to sign for land that may be under water, or completely inaccessible, or that can be reached only after days of travel by horseback.

Coupon-Book-Sales MO

One of the most common of human characteristics is that we all like to get something for nothing. And if that isn't possible, then we all like to get a bargain. It is this appeal to our instinct for bargains that makes the discount house, a legitimate business, so popular.

But there are discount schemes that aren't quite that legitimate. They may not be against the law, but they come very close to stepping across the line.

One type of discount-scheme bunco is the type based on coupon book sales. The venture depends on two factors: the sales ability of the promoter in selling a business on the idea, and his ability to peddle coupon books through itinerant door-to-door salespeople. The usual type of small businesses that are involved are beauty parlors, garages, and service stations.

The bunco operator sets up a small office that he uses as a base from which to call on established businesses. The normal pattern is to select a business that has recently been taken over by a new owner. The pitch is that the bunco operator represents an advertising agency that has formulated a unique plan to help the owner promote his newly acquired business. The owners of the business are reluctant until they learn that this will not require any financing or any cash outlay on their part. The bunco operator simply states that this is an effort on the part of the manufacturer (of a cosmetic, for example) to secure greater distribution and acceptance of his product. Naturally, the store owner will benefit and has been selected by the manufacturer as part of a good-will campaign.

At this time the con man brings out his sample coupon book and explains how it works. Each book has a specific number of coupons, usually ten. The book informs the purchaser of free services that come with a purchase.

Now comes the contract, which specifies the number of booklets to be sold and the number of coupons and the product or service to be offered on each. This is also specified in detail on the contract. The promoter is to print and distribute, at his own expense, the coupon booklets, usually less than five hundred, throughout the neighborhood.

All of this sounds quite legitimate and may actually be the basis of a valid advertising promotion. The business gets none of the proceeds of the sale of the coupon booklets. The contract specifies that all the business owner is to get from the promotion is the advertising and good will the coupon booklets will provide, and nothing more.

The promoters of this type of business are old hands at devising various schemes to guarantee the success of their program. Thus, in a beauty-parlor booklet, they will offer two free shampoos and sets, but the buyer of the booklet will have to buy and pay for five to get the second one free. Or, the booklet may offer a sample under-the-hood car examination with each battery or tire sale. The buyer of the booklet gets caught in several ways. The first is the payment for the booklet, usually as much as the promoter thinks he can get. The second is that the offer in the booklet is usually contingent upon buying a part or a service at full list price.

People who buy booklets of this kind are often entranced by the word FREE printed in large bold letters on each coupon, implying, for example, that the purchaser will get a free front-wheel realignment, oil and filter change, new parts, etc. Very few people bother to read the fine print, and the coupon-book promoter is skillful enough to make his sale and move on to the next victim. Quite often the promoter will have a crew working an entire neighborhood. By the time the purchasers of the booklet have learned how valueless their purchase really is, the promoters will have moved on to another area.

The buyer of the booklet loses a few dollars, but the small businessman who allows his company name to be used as part of this bunco, often creates enough ill will to drive him out of business. The victims do not blame their own desire for a bargain or their willingness to be duped. Instead, they will accuse the owner of the business of shady and shoddy practices.

Operators of the booklet bunco are somewhat like the Williamsons. They will sweep through a neighborhood, swindle as many victims as they can, and then start their operation again in another section.

This scheme is not illegal. Even if the bunco operators are caught, they can always prove they worked with the cooperation and consent of the business owner. They have a contract to prove it. There is nothing illegal in a booklet that uses the word FREE in large, bold letters, but promises nothing. Once again, the law cannot protect people against themselves.

Store Taps

Some bunco schemes are legal; others, of course, are against various laws; some, like the till tap, are outright forms of theft. In a variation of the till tap, the two operators enter a store separately. The first makes a small purchase. Both operators go to the cashier together. The operator that made the purchase will pay for it to get the store owner to open the cash register. After the cash register is opened, the operator will point to some article behind the store owner, indicating that he would want this included in his purchase. When the owner reaches for the article, the operator will insist it isn't the right one and point to some other item of merchandise. But while this exchange takes place, the second operator reaches into the cash register, removes the currency, and leaves the store. Upon seeing the empty cash register the owner often makes a wild dash after the quickly departing thief, and so the second operator has time to clean the register out completely, not omitting all the small change.

There are numerous variations of this basic operation. In one example, the operator making the purchase will drop some small coins on the counter so that they roll off to the back of the counter. He does this after the cash register is open. While the store owner is busily picking up the coins, the other operator removes all cash from the cash register.

The solution is simple for the store owner. Always keep the register shut except when closing a sale. Don't become distracted by anything that takes place elsewhere in the store. The first instinct of the store owner should be to close the register quickly, then investigate.

Any store owner with just himself (or herself) in a store is always at the mercy of a pair of operators or a group. In the case of juveniles, two of them can keep a store owner so distracted and so busy at one end of the store that he will not notice the disappearing merchandise at the other end.

Chapter 5

How to Protect
Your Apartment

Many of the suggestions previously supplied for home protection are applicable to apartments, but the apartment dweller
is just as vulnerable as the home owner, and in some respects,
more so. A general tendency of apartment residents is that they
"do not want to become involved," and so if they see a stranger
at the entrance to an adjacent apartment, they pay little or no
attention on the theory that they are minding their own business. This is a form of rationalization and really means: "I don't
care who gets robbed, so long as I am not the victim."

Those who live in apartments may not have as many windows and doors to secure, but often one of the windows, either
front or rear, exits onto a fire escape. Further, certain areas of
the apartment house—the laundry, the elevators, and inside
garage—have all been the scenes of robberies. And leases often
contain restrictive clauses that do not permit the tenant to

make lock changes or to use alarm systems. But security for an apartment is essential since, on the average, every sixty seconds another apartment is burglarized. You can get insurance, but this will often not cover all of your loss, plus the fact you may lose possessions that have personal significance and cannot be replaced. Also, in some high-crime areas you may be able to get only limited coverage or none at all. In crime areas, it may not be possible to insure furs and jewelry.

If you move into a new apartment, the first thing you should do is to change the front-door lock. Make this a condition of your lease *before* you sign. Some cities now have an ordinance that makes it illegal not to change the lock.

The best kind of lock is one that is equipped with a one-inch deadbolt. The lock should also be the type that has a jimmy-proof vertical drop-bolt rim lock. And get a lock whose manufacturer emphasizes that it is pick-resistant. Finally, the lock should have a double cylinder. A double-cylinder lock is one that requires a key for entry to the apartment, but you must still use a key to get out.

There is a good reason for having a double-cylinder lock. Some apartment doors have thin wooden panels and it is no great effort for a burglar to push these through, reach in, and turn the lock open. But he can't do this if the lock needs an *inside* key. Still another reason is that the burglar, unable to get in the front door, may try and succeed in getting in through a window. But now he has the problem of getting heavy objects out. With the front door locked from the inside, he will be unable to move heavy objects—color TV, stereo equipment, etc. —out of the window. This doesn't mean you won't get "burgled," but it does mean that the burglar's options have become more limited.

A good pick-resistant double-cylinder lock is a step in the right direction, but you are still faced with two problems. With a double-cylinder lock, you effectively lock yourself into your apartment. In the event of an emergency, you may not have time to start a search for your keys. For this type of lock it may be a good idea to keep a spare key, placed somewhere near the door, but out of sight and unlikely to come to the attention of a burglar. Keep this as your "panic" key, your emergency exit key. Another problem with the cylinder lock is that a burglar equipped with a cylinder puller can remove the cylinder in short order. To prevent this you can use a cylinder guard. This is a metal plate that covers the cylinder. It has a circular cut-out in it so that you can still insert your key into the cylinder, and it makes it impossible for the burglar to use his cylinder puller.

Still another security accessory is the brace lock. This consists of a steel rod that extends from your door lock with the other end fitting into a metal socket in the floor. Once the burglar defeats your door lock, his next step will be to push the door open. The brace lock should keep him from doing so, if it is properly installed. If it is loose, the burglar may be able to move the door back and forth enough to pull the lock out of its floor socket.

In older apartment buildings you may find that the wooden door jamb is suffering from old age. Since the door jamb holds part of your lock, it may give way to just several energetic pushes, taking the lock with it. Examine the door jamb. The door should fit right against it, and the screws that hold in the strike should not be loose. These are long, flathead wood screws and those that are missing (and they sometimes are) should be replaced. None of the screws holding the strike in position should be loose; if they are, the screw threads have either rusted or the door jamb has become defective.

Your apartment door should have a peephole. Quite an old ploy is to have someone come to your door claiming they have a package for you and that you must sign for it. The peephole won't let you know if the messenger has a legitimate purpose or not, but at least you can see if the messenger has a uniform, or if there is more than one person. Ask them for the name of their company, and then, without opening the door, get the phone number from the phone book or the operator and verify that you do indeed have a package scheduled for delivery to you. As a further safety check, ask for the name and a short description of the messenger.

If the messenger is indeed someone trying to get into your

apartment he will try to pressure you into opening the door, insisting that he has many deliveries to make and that he doesn't have time. Let him wait.

Nor should you open your door to anyone else, ranging from door-to-door salesmen to service people such as plumbers and electricians claiming to have been sent to you by the management of your building. If you do have a problem in your apartment—a leaky faucet, a window that is stuck, etc.—make sure that you know just who will be sent to your apartment by the building superintendent: that is, the name of the service company and the expected time. Even with these precautions, it is always better to have at least one other person with you at the time the repairs are made.

Make sure you have a lock-type chain on your door. This will enable you to open the door wide enough to allow packages to be slipped in without inviting strangers into your apartment. Even if the person who delivers a package to you isn't a burglar, he can pass along information about the layout and your personal possessions.

The center-swivel latches you will find on your windows supply as little protection in an apartment as they do in a home. If there is a space between the upper and lower window, a burglar can slide a wire through and open this sliding-type latch. If not, he can tape one of the windowpanes, break it with little noise, and then reach in and open the latch. The best type to use on a window is a lock that works with a key. This is an expensive nuisance but it is the only real apartment-window security you can have, other than a switch that turns on an alarm, or lights, or both.

Just because your apartment is a few stories above the street does not mean your terrace door need not be locked. Some burglars are quite athletic and have been known to go from one apartment to another by climbing up, terrace by terrace, trying all doors until they find one that is open. Treat a terrace door just as you would your front door. Use a quality double-cylinder lock, and make sure there is a sturdy deadbolt. Keep an extra key hidden on the terrace. If you lock yourself out, a terrace can become a very uncomfortable place. And, if you have a window facing the terrace, it too deserves a window lock or window lock plus alarm system.

In some states it is against the law to block the exit from a window facing a fire escape. Generally there are restrictions on keeping objects such as plants on the fire escape or outside window sill. The purpose here is for your protection, to let you escape from a fire as easily and quickly as possible. But this lack of clutter also makes it much easier for the burglar. If the fire escape is toward the back of the apartment house, he is less likely to be seen simply because there is less illumination and also fewer people. You cannot put an ordinary metal gate across your window since this would defeat the purpose of the fire escape. But you can now get a gate that has an easily released latch that permits the gate to swing out of the way.

Some burglars prefer apartments to houses. They know how careless people are about front-door locks, so in many cases all they need do is to walk down an apartment-house corridor and try each front door until they find one that is open. A quick ring on the bell soon tells them if anyone is home. If someone is home, they have a convincing story ready. If not, they move quickly into the apartment.

A burglar not only wants to get in, he wants to be sure of being able to get out. And so if he comes in a back window, he may open another window and/or front door to give him a chance for a quick exit. If he comes in through the front door, it is quite likely that even before he starts collecting your possessions, he will open the window that faces the fire escape.

Another reason a burglar may prefer an apartment is that there is a smaller likelihood of occupancy. A house is usually for a fairly large family and is seldom occupied by just one person. On the other hand, there are quite a few apartments that are used by just one person. The average burglar prefers no confrontation at all, but if there is to be a face-to-face meeting, wants the odds in his favor as much as possible. The fewer the people, the better the odds.

In many apartment houses, the management insists on having a master key so that they can get into any apartment, if necessary. It is quite possible you may feel less secure knowing that someone, somewhere, has a key that can open your front door. One way out of this dilemma is to use the lock that is opened by a number arrangement, the type that will open only when numbers are pushed in a certain sequence. The usual combination lock has a fixed number sequence, but the door-lock type (depending on the manufacturer) permits you to select your own combination and to change that combination easily and quickly. Thus, you can have a daytime combination known to your building management. During the day, while you are away at work, they can open your door by using the number series you supplied. At night, though, you can change the combination, and so anyone trying to get in then would not be able to do so. This does mean, however, your apartment is still vulnerable while you are away. Before you make any lock changes, discuss the matter with apartment management. It is also better to do so *before* you sign a lease, not after. Once you sign a lease, you are a captive customer and are certainly not in a good bargaining position. Before you sign the lease, you are a customer; after you sign, you are a tenant. And there's a world of difference between the two.

Still another burglary deterrent is to have two locks on a front door instead of the usual one. These can be two different types, one of which could be jimmy-proof and the other highly pick-resistant. Burglars are as lazy as anyone else and the thought of trying to overcome a double barrier can act as a psychological deterrent. There is also the time factor involved. Most people get in and out of their apartments rather quickly. The sight of someone spending a considerable amount of time in front of a door, possibly making some noise, could arouse concern in some neighbors.

When you buy an alarm system, you will probably get a selfstick label you can affix to the door, stating that the premises are electronically controlled. It might seem strange to use a label such as this on an apartment door, but keep in mind that with every burglar you must try to do three things: (1) You must try to discourage him from trying to enter. The warning label does just that. And so does the sight of a well-protected lock, or the sight of a pair of locks, and a peephole. (2) You must make it as difficult as possible for the burglar to get past the barriers you have erected. (3) Once the burglar is inside, you must make it as uncomfortable and as potentially un-profitable as you can. You can do this by using a system that turns on an alarm and lights, and by not keeping valuables at home or by having them well out of sight and difficult to locate.

If you are not permitted by your lease to install an alarm system or if you don't want the expense at this time, you can still buy the warning label and fasten it to your front door. The burglar may suspect you do not have such a system, but he will not be sure. And that's the point. If it keeps him from entering, it will have achieved its purpose.

Naturally, you can defeat the label by talking or bragging about it. Don't make it the subject of casual conversation and don't confide in anyone. Just put it on your door, forget about it, and let it do its work. And don't let yourself be questioned or cross-examined about it. Your personal security and safety are precisely that—personal.

One of the greatest problems about security is that you must be conscious of it just about all the time. If you have an alarm system in your apartment, you must remember to set it every time you are home and you must test it once in awhile to see if it is working. This can be quite a nuisance, and so after the novelty of having the unit has worn off, you may be inclined to let it go and to forget about it. An alarm system can protect you only if you give it a chance to do so. The same sort of thinking applies to window locks or to any other locks that must be keyed from the inside. The best thing to do is to form the security habit. Set up a routine for yourself so that you check security at night before you retire and each time you leave your apartment. It is the mental effort in remembering the steps to security that is fatiguing, not the steps them-selves. And so, before going to bed at night, check the door and windows. Is the door locked, bolted, and chained? If you use an inside lock with a cylinder, have you closed it with your key? Are your windows key-locked? If you have an alarm sys-tem, is it set to the "on" position?

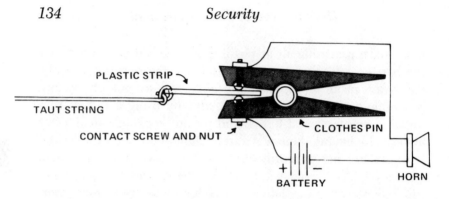

How to make your own pull-trap sensor. Drill holes at the ends of a clothespin and put a 6/32 machine screw (or larger screw) through each hole. Fasten screws with hex nuts. Connect wires as shown to horn and battery. The head of the screws should make contact when the pin is closed. Insert a plastic strip between the screw heads. This strip can be any piece of smooth plastic. Connect a string or wire to plastic and other end of string or wire across area to be protected. When string is contacted by intruder, it pulls the plastic strip away from clothespin. Metal ends of screws contact, closing circuit. Horn blasts and will continue to do so until clothespin is opened or plastic strip inserted again. (Speedex Electronics)

Do you have a flashlight on your night table and if you do, have you checked it to see that it is in working order? Do you have a telephone on your night table (as you should)? Lift the receiver to hear if you get a dial tone. Do you have a lamp on your night table? You should, but if for some reason you cannot, you should have an extension cord with a switch at its end so you can turn on a light elsewhere in the room. Do you have a dog? Some people like to have the dog sleeping across the foot of the bed or on the floor near the bed. Train your dog to sleep across the threshold of your door. Most entries are made through the door and this is where you should have your "canine" alarm.

Dogs in Apartments

Keeping a dog in an apartment for security purposes is an

excellent idea, if you are permitted to do so by your lease, and if you are a dog lover, or at least do not have an antipathy to them. You must also have someone who can take care of your dog if you need to be away all day, and be willing to pay to have a veterinarian check out your dog once in awhile. You must be prepared to accept the trouble and bother associated with taking care of an animal. Now those are a lot of demands on you, but there is a payoff in the form of security.

In an apartment, a dog is a living alarm system and in some respects is better, more secure protection than a dog in a private house. In a private house a burglar can have a direct confrontation with the dog and can soon determine whether the dog poses a threat. Some burglars have a way with dogs and can silence them quickly with food, soothing words, or some heavy instrument if all else fails. But in an apartment the burglar cannot see the dog, does not know whether the dog is a miniature poodle or a German shepherd, and has no way of calming the animal. Once the dog starts barking, that's it. Usually, it isn't the dog the burglar is afraid of, it's the noise.

Certain dogs are specifically trained as "attack" dogs for use in commercial establishments. These dogs are vicious, deliberately made so through intensive training. Most people do not know how to handle such dogs, do not know how to exercise them, and certainly do not know how to control them. They do not belong in an apartment.

Oddly enough, the kind of dog you should get depends on the size of your apartment, and the larger the apartment, the bigger the dog. For a small apartment, consider the advisability of a small dog, such as a small fox terrier or poodle. They can be trained to use a litter box, are economical to feed, become devoted pets, and do not require an undue amount of exercise. They cannot provide you with physical protection and a burglar could probably dispose of them with one well-aimed kick. They are valuable for their bark, for their tendency to yelp and yip at strangers. If you decide to get a dog, don't get a puppy. They may look cute and cuddly, but keep in mind your primary purpose in getting the dog. You are looking for security, not love or affection. Unless you are interested in pedigree, you should concentrate on getting a dog that is trained and is housebroken. There is no reason why your dog should consider your entire apartment as his private bathroom.

A dog that is trained can become untrained. Many people spoil dogs just as some parents spoil children. And so it is sometimes necessary to train the apartment resident as well as his (or her) dog. From time to time it may be necessary for you to take your dog back to the supplier for a refresher course.

The dog should not soil the house, and should not regard all objects within it as his personal playthings. He should be gentle with children and must be able to tolerate the unthinking pullings and pushings of toddlers. If the children are old enough, they must be taught that the dog is a living creature, capable of being hurt and abused.

When you decide to buy a dog, buy from a store or dog supplier with the understanding that the dog is trained. Explain your circumstances, the size of your apartment, the number and age of the occupants, and the approximate amount of time the animal might be left alone. Get all the information you can about the dog *before* you buy: how much food to give the dog, what kind of food, how often to exercise the dog, how to maintain the dog's training, how not to overindulge the dog (a common failing), and how to keep the dog in a peak healthy condition.

Apartment Lighting

Even though you have an apartment, a burglar walking down your corridor looking for a target of opportunity can glance at the bottom of the door and learn if your apartment is lighted or not. If it is about eight o'clock in the evening and there is no light shining under your door, the burglar may immediately consider your apartment as a likely prospect.

For an apartment, as well as for a home, it is helpful to have one or more electric timers that can turn lights on—and off— at the hours you select. If you go out of your apartment and it is dark, or soon will be, and expect to return within an hour or so, do not leave a dark apartment. Don't turn on your foyer light—no one keeps a foyer light burning for any length of time —but do turn on your living-room light. If there is a door between your foyer and your living room, keep the door open so that the light will have a chance to reach the bottom of your front door. If you expect to be away most of the night or all night, use a timer so that the light will turn off at about one o'clock in the morning. A light that remains on all night is as much a signal to a burglar as no light at all.

In addition to lights, turn on a radio set, but keep it playing at low volume. Be careful. Do not do this if you have an old-style tube-type radio. These develop a large amount of heat and can cause a fire. Instead, use a portable, battery-operated transistor radio. These are quite inexpensive and it could be worthwhile getting one, not so much for listening, as for protection. Before you go out, tune it carefully to a station you know will be broadcasting for a number of hours. Adjust the volume so that it can be heard by someone at the door, but not so loud that it will disturb the neighbors. One way of doing this is to put the radio somewhere near the door. This will enable you to keep the volume low and yet let it be heard at the door front by anyone listening there.

Your Front Doorbell

A burglar can easily determine if you are home or not just by ringing your front doorbell. Usually, such a bell is so loud and is so often located near the door that the burglar can hear it quite well. If, after several tries, no one answers, then you've cooperated with him and given him a clear indication that the field is clear.

If possible, relocate your doorbell so its ringing cannot be heard outside the door. If you cannot do this, perhaps you can have it muted somewhat so that it is still inaudible externally. Now, if a burglar pushes your doorbell, he will hear nothing, and will assume of course that your bell is out of order. You might even have a transistor radio playing near the door. In this case the burglar may think you cannot hear the doorbell over the sound of the radio. If your front door has a knocker, have it removed. These make quite a bit of sound and so a burglar can verify if you are home or not. However, as a general rule, burglars usually do not care for knockers because the sound can often carry into an adjacent apartment. For the same reason, they are often reluctant to knock on a door. Both methods make noise, and that is just what the burglar does not want.

Some people turn on a television set instead of a radio as a sound device for protecting their apartment. Unlike a battery-operated transistor radio, television receivers (especially color-television sets) take quite a bit of current from the power line and get quite hot, particularly if the sets are all-tube types, as so many are. They represent a considerable fire hazard and so you should not use them for this purpose. They will also boost your electric bill; a small portable battery-operated transistor radio will not do so.

More About Locks

Locks were discussed briefly in an earlier chapter. Although alarms are important, the lock is probably still your first line of defense against a burglar and perhaps we should review them here. Basically, there are three types of locks, although there are any number of variations of the three. The first is the spring-latch type, also known as a snaplock, which offers no security, but does have the advantage that it will hold a door shut without using a key. But not being forced to use a key means you can forget and leave your key in the apartment.

The restraining part of the spring-latch lock is its V-shaped bolt, usually quite small, extending for approximately a half-inch to about one inch beyond the lock. This doesn't mean that the entire part of this bolt is inside the strike because there is some separation between the end of the door and the strike. Thus, for most spring latches, the amount of bolt inside the strike is quite small.

The second basic type of lock is, you will remember, the combination latch and deadbolt forming a single unit. This type of lock has all the convenience of the spring latch, with some of the security of the deadbolt. The trouble with locks of this kind is that the deadbolt portion of this lock is quite small. After moving the spring-latch V-bolt back with a plastic card, a burglar can use his jimmy to separate the deadbolt from the strike.

The key-operated deadbolt has been recommended as the best, but even here you must be careful. Some deadbolts are quite skimpy. The best deadbolt is one that has large mass; that is, is big, and moves a good distance into the strike. The deadbolt should extend for at least a full inch from its lock when it is opened all the way. If it measures less than this, don't bother. The purpose of a jimmy is to separate the door from the jamb. A jimmy can generally make that separation about a half-inch. A deadbolt that extends for one inch gives you that extra margin of security.

If you have a lock on your front door that has a deadbolt, but doesn't meet this security requirement, you have two choices. The better choice is to leave your existing lock right where it is and install a new lock with a deadbolt having a throw of not less than one inch. Faced by two locks, the average burglar just won't bother. Of course, you'll have the nuisance of requiring two keys, and if you lose just one of them you'll find yourself locked out. Further, you may have some difficulties about this with your landlord, so check with him first. The second choice is to remove your present lock and use the hole cut in your door for the new lock. That's the easy way out and for the burglar may be the easy way in, depending on the lock you buy.

Tamper-Proof Cover

You can get a tamper-proof cover made of metal to fit over the outside portion of your lock cylinder. This will prevent a burglar from using a cylinder puller. The tamper-proof cover is held in place by hard steel bolts (not screws). The cover is inexpensive and adds to your security. Naturally, you only need one for the outside of your lock, not the inside.

Using the Services of a Locksmith

There are all sorts of locksmiths, just as there are all kinds of car mechanics and television repairmen. With a locksmith, though, you literally put your apartment or house in his hands if you buy a lock from him. He has every opportunity, the equipment, and the skill to make duplicate keys to every lock he sells. They are usually honest, though, but it might be your misfortune to select one not quite as honest as he should be. When you visit the store of a locksmith, look in his window and you will find a sign indicating he is a member of some locksmiths' association. He may have a printed sign inside his shop proclaiming his membership. The sign should say also that he is a bonded locksmith. If that is the case, then you will know he has been adequately investigated. Somebody has done a checking job for you.

Special Locks

There are quite a number of lock manufacturers, but if you get a competent locksmith and follow his recommendations, you will probably be taking a big step in the right security direction. However, there are some special locks that do require special mention. One of these is the Chicago Ace Lock. This lock uses a key that has a cylindrical shape. Inside the lock the tumblers are arranged in circular fashion. This makes the lock much more pick-resistant.

Using the cylindrical key of the Chicago Ace Lock has advantages and disadvantages. If you lose the key, the only way to get a duplicate is to get in touch with the manufacturer or one of his authorized service representatives. When you buy a lock of this kind, then, keep a copy of your sales slip. It's a good idea to keep a Xerox copy of the slip in your bank vault and the other among your valuable papers at home.

If you are looking for a lock that has maximum pick resistance, try the Medeco lock. For years they have had a standing offer of a large sum of money, payable to anyone capable of picking their lock. Like the Chicago Ace Lock, the Medeco uses a special key cut in a special way. The keys cannot be duplicated by any locksmith, but only by the manufacturer or his authorized representative. The same precaution about keeping your purchase records applies to this lock also.

Your Key Ring

Since it is inconvenient to have single keys rattling around in your pocket, it is more practical to keep them in a small leather key case. This not only prevents individual keys from getting lost, but keeps the keys from tearing your suit lining. Some people, concerned that they might lose all of their keys at one time with the loss of their key case, very carefully put their name and address inside the case or attach a tag to it carrying the same information. Yes, they will get their keys back, probably delivered personally by a burglar. If you are concerned about losing your keys, make a duplicate set and either keep them in your bank vault or exchange keys with a trusted neighbor or relative. You hold his duplicate set and he holds yours. With favors exchanged this way, there is no obligation, and you are both carrying the burden of trust. But whatever you do, remember not to hide keys outside your home. Burglars are accustomed to looking for keys under doormats, or on top of doors. If you have an apartment, you simply do not have any outside areas for hiding keys.

Your Insurance

If you live in a high-crime area, you may not be able to get insurance for jewelry or furs. A high-crime area is not only one in which there is a great proportion of crimes, but usually includes quite a bit of surrounding territory as well. In some cases you may be able to get only a limited amount of insurance, or the premiums may be extremely high.

Just because you have theft insurance does not mean you will get full payment for the articles stolen. Most possessions depreciate and all you will get will be a percentage of the original cost, assuming you can prove forcible entry. And that's the catch. If, feeling secure because you have insurance, you barge off and leave your apartment door unlocked, or inadequately locked, and a burglar can get in without making so much as a mark on your door, you may have trouble proving theft. An insurance company will demand proof, and there's no better proof than a door that has been forced. The burglar, though, has enough problems of his own without worrying about you, too. He wants to get into your apartment the easiest possible way, without risk, and without work. He isn't going to use a jimmy if he can use a key. He isn't going to use a jimmy if a plastic credit card will do the job.

Chapter 6

How to Make Your Car More Secure

Next to our homes—and often on a par with it—our most prized possession is the automobile. The remark that "Americans have a love affair with their cars" would be more humorous were it not such an accurate statement.

Our romance with the car is due to any number of reasons. Some of us have become exurbanites, and this removal from the city immediately means dependence on the car for shopping, for transportation to the job, and for social activities. We have been so urged by car manufacturers to buy, that not uncommonly many have become two-car families. And the possession of "wheels" is now the great dream of young people.

But the car is not only a great convenience and a pleasure, it is a prime target for all those looking for the easy buck. Just consider the theft opportunity a car presents and compare it with the same opportunities for stealing from a house or apartment. With the house or apartment the thief often does not know whether someone is home or not, and this is a risk he must assume. With the car, there is no such problem, for the thief need merely look in the window. And when he breaks into a home or apartment, the burglar must take a chance on whether or not there is something worth stealing. Yes, there are some burglars who are satisfied with a haul that will net them a few miserable dollars. But for many burglars, such a return isn't commensurate with the risk. With a car, however, any expert car thief can evaluate fairly well what he may expect to get. He can recognize the year and model of the car and a quick look will soon tell him something of its condition. If the paint job is good, if the tires have an adequate amount of tread, if the interior doesn't appear too worn, then the burglar knows almost as much about the car as the owner.

There is one more feature about the car that makes it so attractive a target for theft. Most car-door locks are pathetic. An experienced thief can punch through the car lock almost as fast as its owner can open it. In some cases the thief may not want to do this since he doesn't want to damage "his" property, and so with the help of a coat hanger, is able to release the door, usually in rather fast time. Cars that are illegally parked are opened this way by traffic police, and quite obviously they do not find a locked door much of a barrier. And in many instances, car owners have the habit of slamming their car doors without checking to see if this action has locked the door or not. Similarly, many lock their doors and either leave windows open or else fail to secure side vents.

Consider also that while apartment dwellers may pay some attention to their neighbors, car owners do not even have the slightest interest in any adjacent car. All the car owner wants is to have a parking space, not to have his entrance or exit blocked by other cars, and not to have his car scratched or otherwise damaged. And yet the same man who cleans his car with a lint-free chamois every Sunday casually and unthinkingly exposes his pride and joy to thieves and vandals.

There are probably as many varieties of car thieves as there are house burglars, but you can group them into a few main

categories: (1) the thief who steals to order; (2) the opportunistic thief who steals any car, if you have made it convenient
for him to do so; (3) the car-parts thief; (4) the joyrider who
steals for the satisfaction of having his own wheels, even if for
just a short time; and (5) the vandal, who doesn't actually steal
a car but is simply intent on damaging it.

Stealing to Order

If there is such a thing as an elite class in burglary, the
"steal-to-order" thief is it. By pre-arrangement with a larce-
nous-minded customer (or the thief may be working for a
group), the thief is told to be on the lookout for a particular
model and year of car. He may even be informed of a preferred
color. Once he locates such a car, the thief will stalk it to
learn something of the driving habits of its owner. With this
information on hand, and since the average car is so easy to
enter and drive away, the car thief doesn't find it very difficult
to make delivery.

One of the ways in which the car owner cooperates with the
thief is to leave the registration of the car in the glove compartment. And some owners have the unhappy habit of keeping
a duplicate set of keys in the same place. So now the car owner
may not only lose his car, but has literally given the thief an
invitation to rob his home as well. If, for example, the car is in
a no-pay parking lot, the thief will realize he has just about
enough time to visit the victim's home. Even if the keys aren't
in the glove compartment, the registration does have the name
and address, and quite often that is all that is required.

The thief who gets away with a car on order does have the
problem of supplying a new set of plates and registration. He
can get these from car wreckers. Since we have an individual
state rather than a Federal registration system, it requires no
great effort to transport the car to some other state. Sometimes
the car is shipped to another country. There is a brisk overseas
trade in stolen cars.

Every car has a vehicle identification number. This number

is located in one place in your car where it is easily seen and in another, hidden location. Vehicle ID's can be changed. The car thief does have the problem of locating the hidden number. Car thieves, working as a group, can purchase a late model car of the kind they intend to specialize in, and then strip it, bolt by bolt, until they locate the hidden vehicle identification number. From that point on, they can steal similar model cars with the assurance that they can modify all identification number. Forging registration papers, insurance papers, or any other documents required by the individual states, is comparatively easy. With such a setup in active operation, the car ring is equipped for wholesale theft.

Insurance is part of the reason why car owners cooperate so wholeheartedly with car thieves. What we should realize is that the theft of someone else's car affects all of us. Insurance rates are predicated directly on the number and value of total thefts. If these are high, premiums for theft insurance are correspondingly high, and so even if your car is never stolen, you are still paying for someone else's negligence.

Insurance does *not* mean the insurance company is going to give you enough money to pay for a brand-new model of the car you have been driving. As a car gets older, its value decreases, with the drop in value the greatest amount for the car's first year of life. As a matter of fact, there is a serious drop in value the moment you drive a car out of the showroom. This value decrease does not mean the car is worth less to you, simply that you would get that much less for it in the resale market. Now add to this the fact that theft insurance also includes a certain amount of deductible (the amount the insurance company takes right off the top when evaluating the market worth of your stolen car). And so, what you do get from the insurance company is much less than the value you have mentally put on the car, and may often amount to just enough for you to make a down payment on another car.

There is also another sad corollary to this story. If you bought your car on time payments, you are still responsible for making those payments. The finance company or bank that loaned you the purchase money for the car originally is not responsible for the theft of the car, and does not share with you in its loss. And so now you are in the unenviable position of making payments on a car now in someone else's possession. If your car is stolen, you do not win. You lose, to a greater or lesser degree.

The fact that your car was stolen does not absolve you of responsibility for it. The point is, you are still the lawful owner of the car and if the car is involved in an accident, even if driven by a thief, you can still be sued, and depending on various laws in the individual states, may be forced to pay. And so, even if your car is an old one and its theft is of no great immediate concern, you may still be forced to pay far more than the car is worth.

Your "guilt" in an accident caused by the person who stole your car may be predicated on your contributory negligence. If the thief is driving the car with your car keys and your registration, it would be easy to prove that you practically invited the theft of the car. But if your car is equipped with various devices to hinder or balk car theft, and if you can demonstrate that you did everything humanly possible to prevent the theft, then you may be in a somewhat better legal position.

The Opportunity Thief

Next to homes, automobiles represent the largest single investment made by most American citizens. Yet, most people are notoriously careless with their second most valuable property. According to the National Auto Theft Bureau, in 1970 alone, a rather moderate theft year, some 921,400 cars were stolen in the United States, or one out of every hundred cars registered.

Now, what about opportunity?

Out of all the cars stolen, 76 percent were left unlocked by their owners, and 42 percent, nearly half, even had the keys left in the ignition locks. The opportunistic thief doesn't even need tools. All he has to do is walk through a parking lot, conveniently provided by shopping centers, or along any typical residential street, look inside the parked cars, and quickly try the doors.

Most stolen cars are eventually returned to their owners, but statistics on their return do not carry the whole story. In many instances valuables inside the car disappear, never to be found, or the trunk is forced open to yield its contents. Some people even put valuables in the glove compartment. Any self-respecting thief can dispose of the lock on that compartment very quickly, assuming the lock is used by the owner; most often it is not. The 16 percent of the cars that are never returned represent an annual loss of over 140 million dollars. Even when the vehicles are recovered, they may very well have been stripped.

The "Car-Parts" Thief

Don't take it personally, but some thieves think more about your various car parts than they do about the entire car. There are basically two kinds of car-parts thieves. One is the thief who has a car model identical to yours and needs parts for his car, parts he is either unable or unwilling to buy. He may not only strip your car of various accessories, but may take others as well to keep an inventory on hand just in case he should ever need them.

The second type of car-parts thief makes a specialty of stealing car parts. In some instances he can earn as much for these parts as he could for the entire car, but with much less risk. Automobile tires, grilles, front fenders, hoods, bumpers, and batteries do not carry identification numbers and so for these items the thief can find a ready market.

The Joyrider

The joyrider is mostly a young male, although some young females are getting into this scene. The joyrider may have his own car, but may take yours on impulse, just to "try it out," or he may be on a date and wants to make an impression, or he may have neither a car nor a license but is absolutely convinced he is tops as a driver. Whatever the reason may be, your car will disappear for a number of hours and during that time will be in the possession of someone with little driving experience, willing to take risks, prone to driving at high speeds, and inclined to operate the car using driving techniques that will do the car no good. Jack-rabbit starting (burning rubber) is just one example.

Oddly, most car thieves are not professionals, but amateurs. And about two-thirds of these amateurs are teenagers. What you are up against is a young kid who is out to take whatever he can and who has absolutely no thought for the consequences. And since he cannot or will not think ahead, he will take the first car that is readily available. For the teenager an available car is one whose door is left open with a key in the ignition. There is no real reason for him to break into a car when there are so many available without effort.

Note this combination: unlocked door and key in the ignition. But if you lock the door and leave the key in the ignition, then you are in even greater trouble, for now you have put irresistible temptation in the path of the teenager thief. His reaction is predictable. He'll smash the side-vent window with whatever he has available—a brick, an empty Coke bottle, a hammer handle, anything. And then he is in and away in a moment.

The problem with the joyrider thief isn't that you won't get your car back. You probably will. But it may no longer be recognizable. The joyrider thief is highly accident prone, firmly believes he is invulnerable as long as he is behind the wheel of a car, and may very well be aware that he is a juvenile and so will be treated leniently if caught. He may also realize that the average car owner may be so delighted to get his car back that he may not be willing to press charges.

The Vandal

Next to the teenager joyrider, the vandal may very well be the worst of the car thieves. He is really not a thief; generally he is someone ranging in age from the teens to the mid-twenties who enjoys destruction. He will bend your whip antenna out of shape or may bend it back and forth until it breaks and then walk off with it. Or, he may take a stick with a nail protruding from its end, and then walk along a line of cars scratching the paint. Or, he may slash tires. Or, smash windows. He doesn't steal, but he can do as much damage as a thief. The problem with the vandal is that his behavior is so senseless it is unpredictable. And while a car can be protected, at least to some extent, against a thief, there isn't too much you can do about the vandal. We now have antennas that can be recessed to prevent someone breaking them off, but there are no slash-proof tires or scratch-proof paints.

How to Protect Your Car

There are a number of ways of protecting your car and a variety of commercial devices available, but just as a house or apartment can be invaded by a very determined thief, so too is your car vulnerable to someone who has made up his mind to steal it. However, there are some important factors in your favor. One of these is that the thief is just as disinclined to work as anyone else and so will pass up a car that obviously has some protection in favor of one that looks like "easy pickings." Another factor is that the car thief, like the apartment or house burglar, likes to work in privacy and preferably in the dark. The need for privacy and darkness, though, is gradually giving way as thieves are beginning to realize that most people aren't interested in activities involving someone else's car—just so long as it isn't their own.

Here is a list of things you can do to protect your car:

· Do not leave your car key in the ignition. And don't take the key out of the ignition and put it in the glove compartment. Take the key with you and make sure it does not go out of your possession. Do not keep your car keys—and that means ignition and trunk keys—on the same key chain as your regular house and office keys. It is much too easy to hand a parking attendant your entire key chain. When parking in a commercial parking lot, leave your ignition key only. Remove your trunk key from your automobile key ring before driving into the commercial parking lot.

- When buying a car, many factors should influence your decision. Consider that from the viewpoint of car security it is better to buy a car whose doors must be locked with a key. Cars you can lock just by pressing a button and then closing the door offer less protection. Also, if you must lock the door, you are less likely to leave the key in the ignition. Make sure you have two sets of car keys, ignition and trunk, and let your wife hold the second set. In this way, if you do leave your car keys in the ignition but lock the door you can arrange to have the door opened quickly to retrieve your keys. Keys in the ignition present a most tempting target.
- Don't leave your registration in the car, and if the laws of your state also require other papers, such as an identification card or proof of insurance, keep them in your wallet. The only papers you should have in your glove compartment are those the laws of your state require.
- Don't assume your driveway is a safe parking area just because it belongs to you. Your car can be stolen from your driveway just as easily as from the street. Put your car in your garage. And don't leave the garage door open. Do this even if you are planning to use the car again at some later hour. When your car is in the garage, behave as though your car were out in the street. This means closing all car windows, making sure the vent windows are closed and latched, that the ignition key is in your pocket, and that all doors to the car are locked. A car door that is shut isn't necessarily locked. If your garage has a window, keep it closed with a key-type window lock.
- If you have more than one car and you have just a single-car garage, park the less desirable car directly in front of the garage door, and not out in the street.
- The only things of value you should keep in your car trunk are your spare tire and the tools you need for chang-

A car parked in a driveway or carport isn't automatically protected. The best place for a car, from a security viewpoint, is inside a locked garage. If the garage door has window glass, this means you need a keyed lock inside as well as outside. There is no protection if a thief can break a pane of glass and then just reach inside and turn a handle to open the door.

    ing a tire. A car trunk is easy to open. However, if you are out on a trip, hide everything you can in the car trunk. This doesn't mean it is safer in the trunk, but at least the thief will not know whether it is worth his while to make an effort to open the trunk. If he sees merchandise all over the car seats, just waiting to be stolen, he may accept your kind invitation. If you have merchandise in your car, covering the goods with a newspaper or old blanket is futile. You can be sure the burglar is aware that you are as lazy as he is.

· If you have an electric pencil, mark your name somewhere on a hidden metal surface of your car. This can be inside the door, on the rear of a bumper, or inside the hood. If you don't have an electric pencil, use a sharp-edged tool such as an awl or pick or even a screwdriver.

· If you are planning to buy a new car, become security-conscious. Give preference to a car that requires a key for locking the door, that has a steering column lock, that has a buzzer to remind you that the car key is still in the ignition, that has no vent windows.

· If you are planning to buy a used car, keep in mind that

if you buy the car from an individual you must return the car to its original owner if it is stolen. The responsibility is yours. Be careful about ads placed by individuals offering to sell a car at what seems to be a tremendous bargain. This is one way in which thieves dispose of cars. However, if you buy a used car from a dealer, then it is the dealer's responsibility to make sure he doesn't sell you a stolen car. If he does, and it is repossessed, you are entitled to a refund.

· Try not to park your car in known high-crime areas.

· When parking, try to park your car in the most lighted area.

· Operators of open-air parking lots are generally not responsible for the security of your car. The extent of any possible responsibility varies from state to state, but you can safely assume it doesn't exist. Nor are open-air parking-lot operators responsible for the contents of your car, and that includes the trunk.

· It is better to park in an open-air parking lot than out on the street; it is better to use an indoor parking building than an open parking lot.

· A dog in a car is good security but may be tough on the dog. If the day is hot and the car is parked where the sun can reach it, this would be an act of inhumane cruelty. Use a dog when you plan to be away a short time.

· If your car becomes disabled while you are traveling, stay with the car. Hang a large white handkerchief from the antenna of your car. This is now generally being recognized as a car-distress signal. Try to get your car towed to a garage as soon as possible. You may regard towing rates as very high, but these rates are much cheaper than having your car completely stripped. Strippers can cannibalize your car almost as rapidly as a thief can steal it. An obviously abandoned car is a direct invitation to theft.

· Think twice about installing a cartridge player or a CB unit in your car. These are highly desirable items and represent quick cash and a ready market for the thief. You can get mounting brackets that make these items difficult to remove. Beware of cartridge-player and CB mounts that can be installed in just a matter of minutes. They can be removed just as quickly.

· When parking your car, whether in a parking lot, garage, or out in the street, never let it be known how long you will be gone. Some parking attendants do ask, so make your answer: "Not long." If you must park in an open parking lot, try to select one that has just a single entrance and exit. If you use the lot regularly, get to know the attendant's name and use it every time you park. Mention your own name. Sooner or later, despite the large number of cars parked, he will associate you, your name, and your car.

· Do not leave your car parked overnight in an airport parking lot. These are open-air types, are rarely fence enclosed, often have several entrances and exits, and are so large that no attendant could possibly remember you or your car. A thief can drive in a piece of junk that can barely move, pick up a parking ticket, and then use that ticket for driving out with your car.

· The best place for your car at night is in your own locked garage.

· If you commute to and from a bus or train, always park your car in company with other cars and not by itself off in some odd corner of the parking lot. Yes, your car is more likely to get scratched or otherwise damaged by other parkers, but it is also less likely to be stolen.

Anti-Theft Accessories

There are quite a number of anti-theft accessories you can use for your car, none of which will actually prevent a car from being stolen. However, the more difficult you make the job of theft, the less likely it is that your car will be stolen. There is no reason for a thief to spend two hours trying to take your car when the car immediately adjacent to yours can be had in a matter of minutes. The accessories for a car are quite similar to those for a house or apartment.

Interior Knobs

It is most likely that your car has a flanged doorknob on the inside, both on the driver's side and the passenger's side. This makes it easy for you to open the door, and almost as easy for a thief. All he must do is to work a length of stiff wire metal —a coat hanger does the job very well—past the rubber gasket of the window. With the end of the wire fashioned in the form of a hook that can engage the flanged doorknob, the thief can open your door quite easily. Once he is inside your car, no one will pay much attention to him. The only pressure he will experience is your possible unexpected return.

Not only thieves, but policemen as well, use this technique for removing cars that are illegally parked. Once your car is towed away, the penalty is quite often a rather stiff fine.

To minimize this action, you can replace your present interior flanged-type door handles with round knobs. This does make it a bit more difficult for you to open your car doors, but it also is a theft deterrent.

Wheel Locks

Tire thieves don't bother just stealing tires—they take the entire wheel. And so what you lose is the hub cap, tire, and wheel. Multiply this by four and the replacement cost can easily be several hundred dollars. In some instances the thieves, who usually work as a team, aren't all that gentle in lowering the car to the ground, and so you may have some damage to pay for as well.

But that isn't all. Car strippers, seeing the car minus its wheels, may very well assume that the car has been abandoned, and so will be over and through your car like a horde of locusts, removing the battery, radio, generator, windshield wipers, and anything else having some possible use or resale value.

But that isn't all. Your car is now stripped and apparently abandoned. But its windows are still intact and to some teenagers this is an intolerable situation. They remedy this easily with just a few well-aimed rocks. In the short time you were away, your car could have been reduced to a useless pile of junk. To add insult to injury, you may have to pay to have it towed away, depending on the municipal laws and ordinances of your town or city.

To avoid starting on this chain of events, you can equip each of your wheels with a wheel lock. The wheel lock replaces one nut on each wheel. Get a set of four so you can have one for each wheel. However, even with wheel locks you will still be faced with a problem. You must always be sure to have the wheel-lock key with you when you drive. If you get a flat tire and you do not have the wheel-lock key with you, then you must begin removing the lock forcibly—and that in itself can be quite a job. Don't be tempted into leaving the wheel-lock key in your glove compartment or behind the sun visor. Those are exactly the places the thief will look for them. The best thing to do is to give your wife or some other member of the family a duplicate key, or to keep a duplicate key at home in a location known to other members of your family. In that case, a telephone call may help solve your flat-tire problem.

Battery Lock

Some thieves specialize in the theft of batteries, for these can be readily sold in the used-battery market. Stealing a battery is a theft that can be done in just a few minutes, and to those who walk by, it does look as though the driver is simply having some engine trouble. The thief just lifts the hood, disconnects the battery terminals, and then raises the battery up and out.

Without the battery, of course, your car just isn't going anywhere. This means you will probably have to pay for towing plus the cost of a new battery. In some cases, cars that have been stripped this way have also received overtime parking tickets.

To protect the battery you can equip it with a battery lock. Generally, once a thief lifts the hood and sees the battery lock he will move on to another car not so equipped. Why should he work, possibly attract attention and run any kind of risk when there are so many cars with batteries, readily available, and equally ready to be removed?

Hood Lock

The trouble with the battery lock is that it protects just this one car component. A thief that lifts your car hood may not only walk away with the battery, but the generator as well. With the hood lifted, it is easier for him to jump the ignition and get the car started. A hood lock can minimize this risk, but the trouble with hood locks is that they usually look so unattractive.

Steering-Wheel Lock

You can get a steering-wheel lock that fastens the wheel to the brake or to the gear shift. One type of lock consists of a long metal bar running between the wheel almost to the floor board. It can be a nuisance to unlock and to store, but it will protect your car. Before stealing a car, a thief with at least some experience will look inside your car. If he sees a steering-wheel lock it is probable he will be sufficiently discouraged to move on to another car not so equipped. The advantage of a steering-wheel lock is that even if the thief manages to jump the ignition, he is just not going to go anywhere, at least not in your car.

The steering-wheel lock, the hood lock, and the various other component locks all present problems to a greater or lesser degree. You can drive if you lose your wheel-lock key or your battery-lock key, but not if you misplace the key to the steering-wheel lock. It will take hours with a hacksaw to cut through a steering-wheel lock.

Tape-Deck Lock

If you haven't as yet installed a tape deck in your car, but plan to do so, get one that comes with a built-in lock. If not, then be sure to get a lock. Tape decks are highly popular items with car thieves. Quite often this is the only part of your car the thief will be interested in since there is a readily available used tape-deck market, making it very easy for the thief to dispose of any tape decks he steals.

Ignition Switch

You can install a switch that connects in series with your regular ignition switch. This means both switches must be turned on before the car will start. Since the supplementary security ignition switch is so easy to use—you just push it with your finger—quite obviously its value lies in the skill with which you can hide it from the thief. Unfortunately, there aren't too many places in a car where things can be hidden. You can put the switch under the dashboard or in the glove compartment, but those are two places the thief will be sure to look. Further, an experienced thief can trace the ignition wires quite easily.

Still, the supplementary ignition switch is helpful. If you leave your keys in the ignition, no opportunity-type thief is going to bother with your car once he tries the regular ignition key and sees that it does not start the car. Also, many thieves limit the amount of time they will spend in stealing a car, thinking that the longer they are in the car the greater the chances of detection.

Of the 950,000 or more cars that are now stolen each year, some 76 percent of these thefts will be due to keys being left in the ignition. That is why some of the newer cars have an alert alarm or buzzer to remind the driver to take his ignition keys with him.

Another type of supplementary ignition switch, the Auto Guardian, makes it virtually impossible to start your car, even with the key in the ignition. The Auto Guardian is a solid-state, subminiaturized electronic system designed specifically to prevent auto theft. Unlike other types of supplementary ignition switches, this component is mounted directly on the dash. It consists of a small rectangular panel containing the numbers 0 through 9 and is programmed for a four-digit number combination that is exclusively yours. You must touch each digit on the keyboard, in the right combination, to allow the ignition system to operate. Your car will start only if the correct code is used. Yes, someone can guess the code, but the odds against guessing the combination are over 36,000 to 1. To start your car, you must first push the numbered keyboard digits in the correct sequence and then use your regular ignition key.

Car-Equipped or Self-Equipped?

When you buy your next car, should you get one that is security-equipped or is it better to do your own? There are advantages and disadvantages to both methods. The security-equipped car saves you the trouble of getting and installing various security devices; but if these are available as options you will be paying top dollar for them. However, they will save you the time and trouble of doing your own installation or having someone do it for you. If you trade in the car, they may add to the value of the trade-in, but you usually cannot remove these built-in gadgets for your new car.

If you decide to install your own security methods, you have an opportunity to shop for devices that will give you the maximum protection at the lowest purchase and installation cost. Further, you will not have to accept what the car manufacturer

Two types of electrical switches. The one at the left is an electrical plunger type used for car protection. The auto door, hood, or trunk circuit is completed when the button is released. The switch at the right is a key type. A protective circuit is actuated when the lock switch is operated by the key. (On-Guard)

supplies, but can select those devices that seem to offer the greatest security. You can also remove them for use in your new car if you decide to sell your old one. Installing your own car-security measures does mean you must shop and spend time in installing, or paying someone to do it for you. Auto-security manufacturers offer a variety of do-it-yourself kits that contain complete instructions, hardware, necessary wire, plus any accessory materials.

Auto Alarms

It might seem that one of the best ways to protect your car would be to install an alarm system, somewhat similar in concept to the alarm setup in your apartment or house. But before you do so, you should be aware that in some areas a car alarm must shut off automatically, and is required to do so by law. A thief may set off your alarm and be frightened away by it, but you may get a ticket for violating an anti-noise law. Consider these possible case histories:

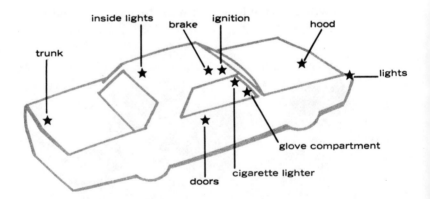

Various areas or points in a car that can be used with a "change-of-state" sensor. If the glove compartment is opened, for example, this could actuate a sensor that, in turn, would trigger an alarm. The hood, trunk, and doors are more commonly located sites for sensors, but the brake, inside lights, cigarette lighter, or glove compartment can also be used.

1. You have parked your car, set your car alarm, and gone to a movie. A thief, attempting a robbery, trips the alarm system and is frightened away by it. Yes, the burglar is foiled, but by the time you return to your car, your battery may be dead, or so weak you are unable to start your car.

2. You have parked your car, set the car alarm, and are off shopping. A thief opens your car hood, trips the alarm, and is frightened away by it. The screaming alarm, though, has attracted some residents in that area who promptly blame you (in absentia) for the continuous noise (and not the thief who tripped the alarm). In exasperation, they cut wires left and right under your hood in an effort to stop the alarm. Once they accomplish this, they leave, but the hood may still be open. This attracts opportunistic thieves who walk away with your car battery.

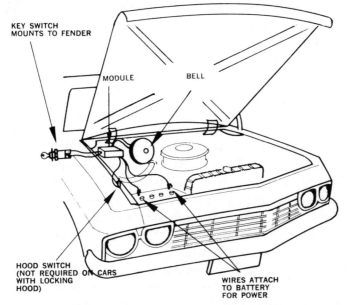

KEY SWITCH
MOUNTS TO FENDER

MODULE   BELL

HOOD SWITCH
(NOT REQUIRED ON CARS
WITH LOCKING
HOOD)

WIRES ATTACH
TO BATTERY
FOR POWER

Diagram of auto-alarm installation. The unit is set to its "on" or protective mode by a key switch mounted on a fender. The car battery supplies the power for the alarm. The module contains circuits for recycling the alarm, turning it off and on for predetermined amounts of time. The hood switch turns the system on when the hood is lifted just an inch or two. (Speedex Electronics)

To prevent either of these possibilities install a timer. Select one that will cut off your alarm in several minutes and automatically reset the alarm some minutes later.

Siren Recycler

Many auto alarm systems were sold prior to the establishment of anti-noise ordinances. Since, in some areas it is now against the law to have continuous alarm operations, you can modify your present alarm system if it is this type by inserting a siren recyler. This will fit all makes of siren alarms, both the relay and solid-state sensor types. In case of alarm, a recycler will shut the siren off after five minutes and will then automatically re-arm the system, thus offering protection from renewed intrusion.

One other caution: If you have an alarm system, prominently display the telephone number at which you can be reached, so that local police can reach you by phone if the alarm is triggered. In some areas the law requires that the alarm be capable of automatic shutoff and that you have your phone number displayed where it can be readily seen.

There are many kinds of alarms and they make all sorts of sounds. You can get a buzzer, a bell, or a siren (either continuous tone or whooping). You can get an alarm that sounds only if the doors are opened, or a type that will protect the doors, the hood, and the trunk. Usually an alarm is triggered or set off by any opening that disturbs a dormant electrical system. Alarms can also be activated when a thief opens the glove compartment, depresses the brake pedal, turns on the car lights, or uses the cigarette lighter. The car owner can use a secret switch or dash keylock to activate the alarm. Generally, there is a time delay so the car owner can get to the switch and disable it. Of course, if the owner forgets to turn off the alarm switch he will be reminded about it quite loudly.

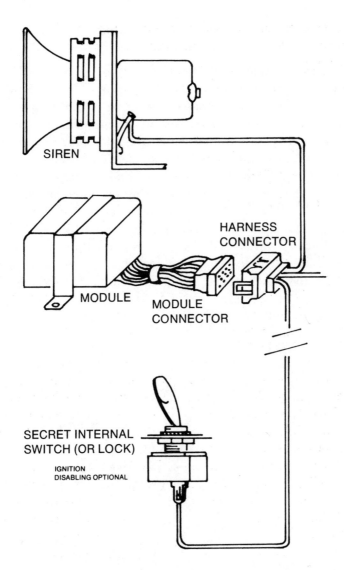

SIREN

HARNESS
CONNECTOR

MODULE   MODULE
CONNECTOR

SECRET INTERNAL
SWITCH (OR LOCK)

IGNITION
DISABLING OPTIONAL

One possible arrangement for an auto alarm system. The secret switch can be located somewhere under the dash. Turning on the switch when leaving the car sets the alarm system in its "on" position and may also disable the ignition. The module contains circuits for delaying the alarm turn-on, to give the car owner time to close the car door. The module also turns the alarm on if a thief tries to gain entry at various points, or touches various parts of the inside of the car. It also recycles the alarm, turning it off after a certain amount of time, and then on again.

Alarm systems can also be used for recreational vehicles, campers, motor and trailer homes, and boats. Some come equipped with a test/panic button to indicate an emergency condition or to test the alarm. Alarms are generally twelve-volt types and operate from a standard car battery.

Some auto thieves will try to defeat the alarm system by jacking up the front wheels and towing the car to some location where an alarm can go on and stay on until the burglar manages to defeat it. A car can be rolled up an inclined plane right into a waiting truck, or else hoisted by its front wheels and towed away. To defeat this technique you can use a pendulum switch. When any door, hood, or trunk is opened or when the car is moved, the pendulum switch will close a pair of contacts, sending current to the alarm. Not all alarm systems are equipped with a pendulum switch and so not all offer this additional protection.

Many thieves do not like to work under the conditions imposed by an activated alarm. Yet, some burglars are highly persistent. If they can manage to get into the car fast enough, they may be able to find the alarm switch or else cut the wires leading to it. There are some types of alarms that cannot be

Car thief may find this protection method somewhat unexpected. Flexible switch beneath seat turns on alarm. Switch can also be arranged so that pressure of thief's body turns strip switch off. If strip switch is in series with ignition switch, car will not start. (Tapeswitch Corp.)

defeated by cutting wires. Once the alarm switch is closed, a module containing solid-state circuitry is activated, making the alarm independent of the switch. Also, some alarm switches are wired in series with the ignition switch. But the car will not start unless the alarm switch is turned on, creating precisely the condition the thief does not want. The car owner, however, can defeat the alarm switch, and so can start the car without sounding the alarm.

When to Protect Yourself

Many car owners install some form of security system after they have been robbed. Someone who loses a battery, or wheels, or a tape unit, has the idea of security forcibly brought home. But after the anger subsides and the security system is installed the usual let-it-go attitude prevails once again. Car doors are left unlocked, keys remain in the ignition system, and the entire pattern of carelessness and theft is repeated. No lock is worth the room it takes up unless it is used. No alarm system is worth carrying around in your car unless it is in working condition, ready for action. Thieves may be lazy but the one great factor working in their favor is that they are no more so than the ordinary individual.

Car-Parking Check List

1. Have you parked your car in a well-lighted area?
2. Have you removed personal property and packages from seats and floors and locked them in the glove compartment and/or trunk?
3. Is the ignition locked? Is the steering wheel locked? Do you have your keys with you?
4. Are all windows locked? Rolled up completely? Side vents secure?
5. Do you have the burglar-alarm system switched on?
6. Is the hood locked?

Protecting Your Gasoline Supply

There are three types of car thieves: those who want your entire car; those who want some part of it, such as your stereo unit, or your battery; and the least demanding of all, the gasoline thief. All he wants to do is to siphon the gasoline out of your tank into his, or, more usually, into some sort of container.

One way you can protect yourself from gasoline theft is to use a keyed gas cap. These are made for various makes and models of cars and an automobile supply house should be able to sell you one. These locking gas-cap devices require a key to open, but not to close. To lock such gas caps, just press down on them when they are in position and the device will lock automatically.

When you buy such a security device, the key will probably be marked "gas." This will help you identify it at once since you will need to open the lock when you buy gasoline. If the key isn't so marked, it would be helpful if you did so. Keep the key on the chain immediately adjacent to your ignition key. You'll need both to go anywhere.

Keyless gas guard consists of tempered steel spring that fits into gas-tank-filler neck. It prevents gas siphoning, but permits filling at a gas station. (Imageast, Inc.)

Another type of gasoline-protection device is the keyless gas guard, or anti-siphon guard. This consists of a coiled spring that screws into the gas-tank-filler neck in seconds and cannot be easily removed. It allows easy filling at the gas station, but restricts entry of a siphon. The unit is made of tempered steel and is universal—that is, it will fit any car.

Temporarily or Permanently Stolen?

If your car is stolen, whether or not you will get it back depends in part on the kind of thief who made away with it. About half of all car thefts are attributed to juveniles who want a car, want it now, and don't care whose car it is. These cars are usually recovered, since the thief abandons the car as soon as it runs out of gas. Whether or not the car will be damaged is quite another matter. Some juveniles are much better thieves than they are drivers. Since part of their enjoyment is in risk taking, the odds are against your getting the car back without some damage.

The easiest car to steal is the convertible: a simple cut through the soft fabric and the thief has his hand right inside the car. All it takes is a sharp razor mounted in a holder, such as those designed for using the razor as a scraper. The next easiest is the older style of car that has a small side or vent window. They have rubber seals. The burglar inserts a screwdriver between the seal and the frame and can often lift the window enough to get at the side latch. If not, he uses a wire coat hanger and works it in until it catches on the latch.

The Warning Alarm Sticker

When you buy an alarm system for your home or for your car, you will get a self-stick label announcing that the premises or the car are protected by an alarm. If you do get such a label with your home alarm system, use it, and be sure to mount it where a prospective burglar can see it. But if you get such a label with your car alarm system, do *not* use it.

This may sound contradictory, but there are good reasons for this kind of action. With a home alarm system the burglar has no way of getting at the alarm. He doesn't know what kind it is, doesn't know if you mean the door is protected, the windows, or all of the house. He doesn't know if you have an ultrasonic alarm, a radar alarm, whether you are area or object protected. And because he doesn't know, it is quite likely he will move on to a less security-minded prospect.

Now consider your car. You have a sticker on it saying the car is alarm protected. There's no question about the kind of system it is and the thief knows it. He can get under your car, quickly locate the wiring to the alarm, cut the wires, and that's the end of your protection. With a car alarm system the best thing to do is to keep the thief guessing. Do you have an alarm or don't you? This is one of the thoughts in his mind, and you can be sure he is prepared to make a quick getaway the moment he hears an alarm.

On many car alarm systems, the lock for the alarm is mounted in an easy-to-get-at position. There is a reason for this. It is convenient for the car owner to be able to set the alarm with a key, and so the alarm lock is mounted in some conspicuous spot. This is equivalent to notifying the thief that the car is alarm protected, and performs the same function as the alarm sticker or label. Knowing the car is equipped with an alarm, the thief can take steps to disable it. Further, by positioning the alarm lock where it can be readily seen, you have, in effect, also told the thief where he must reach in to cut to disable the alarm system.

There is still one other serious disadvantage to the alarm label and the visible alarm lock. Many thieves reason that only the owner of a car containing valuables would go to such trouble or expense. Of course, they could be wrong but this won't stop them from making an attempt at your car. If they can disable your alarm system, having been alerted by you that such an alarm exists, then your car becomes more desirable than some other vehicle that may or may not have an alarm.

If you do have an alarm system in your car, don't expect it to do the impossible. An alarm is no guarantee that your car won't be stolen. All it does is assure you that there may be some noise from your car siren. But if you have your car parked at some remote corner of a parking lot, and some of them are tremendous, the wail of your siren will be ignored. It's your car, your property, and no one is going to run a great distance across some car-parking area to get involved in a possible clash with a thief. If you are going to park, try to get as close to the entrance as possible. This is where you will find the parking attendants. Or else select a parking lot that is small. And if you park out in the street, try to park near a house or store with some activity. Park in a deserted street, adjacent to a vacant building, and all that will happen is that your siren will scream until the thief can get at the connecting wires. Car alarms have limitations and are valuable only if you recognize these limitations and work within them.

The Time-Delay Protector

One of the best car-protection devices is inexpensive, simple, and extremely effective: a time-delay fuse connected to the spark coil. The thief gets into your car, starts the ignition, and is able to drive a short distance, usually less than a block, and then the time-delay fuse opens. The car stops and there is the thief, with a car that won't move, away from the safe and quiet area where you had parked your car. He is now out in open traffic, where at any moment a policeman may come along to find out why the car is blocking traffic with, of course, the usual request for a license and/or registration.

An even better arrangement is to have an alarm go off, not when the thief first enters your car, but after it has stalled out in traffic due to the opening of the time-delay fuse. You have now put the thief in a most awkward position, and he does the only thing he can do under the circumstances. He runs.

Your Other Vehicles

How to Protect Your Motorcycle

The trouble with protecting motorcycles is that just about

none of the security features used for automobiles can be applied to the problem. A pair of thieves, working as a team, can literally pick up a motorcycle, put it in a van or truck, and drive off with it. And if the motorbike has an alarm, so what? Covered with a blanket in the van, completely enclosed by the walls of the van, the muffled sound it will emit won't attract attention.

About the only solution is the use of a chain and a lock. This does not mean the ordinary bicycle chain that can be snipped. It does mean the heaviest, most solidly forged chain you can get and a tough, case-hardened padlock. And the post you wrap the chain around must be equally tough. Don't pick a small tree and think you are safe. A thief can saw through that rather quickly.

If you park your motorcycle in your own garage, at least make sure the doors cannot be forced open. If you have any doubts, chain-lock your motorcycle just as though you had parked it out in the street.

Keep a record of your motorcycle identification number, the manufacturer, model number, and year. Use an electric pencil to mark your identification on it in at least two places, preferably spots that aren't readily noticeable. Keep your bill of sale to prove the motorcycle is yours. And make sure your theft-insurance premiums are paid.

Many of the precautionary rules for cars apply to motorcycles. Don't park on deserted streets, or in high-crime areas, or in the remote end of a parking lot. If possible, don't park at all, and if you do, at least try to put the motorcycle where you can keep an eye on it. Yes, this does destroy the fun of owning a motorcycle, but theft destroys the fun of everything else as well.

How to Protect Your Bicycle

Bicycles are now enjoying renewed popularity. As a result, bicycle sales have been booming, and many new styles and models have been introduced. At one time bicycles were relatively inexpensive, but with the addition of special bicycle features, such as gear shift and brakes, some have moved up to a hundred dollars or more, making them particularly tempting targets. Bicycle thefts have kept pace with the burgeoning bicycle market.

To leave a bicycle unattended and unlocked is simply an invitation to theft. All the thief has to do is mount it and ride away.

The most common method of securing a bicycle is to use a key-type padlock and a length of chain, ordinarily about three feet long. The chain is often enclosed in a plastic sleeve to protect the bicycle paint finish against chain scratches. This system supplies a moderate amount of security, but with some negative factors.

The first of these is the device to which you fasten the bicycle chain. If this is a pole, for example, and the pole is short enough, all the thief has to do is to lift the bicycle and chain over the pole. It is true the chain will still be attached to the bicycle, but then the thief can remove the bicycle to some remote area where the chain can be hacksawed off.

A thief can hacksaw his way through most chains, so if you are going to use a chain, get the strongest and toughest one you can buy. Chains come in various degrees of thickness and hardness, so the amount of security you will have will depend on these qualities. The lock is also important. Just because a lock closes doesn't mean it can't be opened by being smacked with a hammer. The sturdier the lock, the more it will cost.

Percentagewise, security for a bicycle is more expensive than for most other forms of transportation. It is possible to buy a bicycle for eighty dollars and to spend about sixteen dollars for protection. This is 20 percent of the original cost. Comparably, for a car costing four thousand dollars, this would mean spending eight hundred dollars.

Whether an attempt will be made to steal a bicycle depends also on where you park it. In a high-crime area, any bicycle left parked for one day will certainly be subjected to one or more "theft tests." This means that one or more thieves will try to steal the bicycle. Whether they will be able to do so or not depends entirely on how the bicycle is protected. Not even with an automobile do you have such assurance that thieves will try to get away with your property.

At one time, bicycle thieves relied on heavy-duty, specially made hacksaw blades to cut through bicycle chains. Today they have the services of a link cutter that does the job faster and easier. Whether the chain link cutter will be successful or not depends on the size of the link cutter and the size and strength of the chain.

To minimize the possibility of bicycle theft, manufacturers now offer various chain-and-lock combinations, designed to resist sawing or cutting. One of these, known as Kryptonite, is a clever arrangement of metal baffles that put the bolt of the padlock out of the reach of bolt cutters. And, instead of a chain, this unit uses a thick metal band to hold the frame and wheel of the bicycle against a parking meter, or a post. The bonnet that protects the padlock shackle from being cut or forced open is made of stainless steel.

Some bicycles are made with a removable front-wheel feature. This doesn't relieve the owner of the necessity for chaining the bicycle. After doing so, he removes the front wheel and takes it with him. There is no question that this is an additional deterrent, and it eliminates the possibility of the thief riding away with the bicycle. But it is a nuisance, and it does mean an assembly and disassembly job every time the bicycle is parked.

Bicycles aren't licensed, so there is no bicycle identification number you can use to prove a particular stolen bicycle is yours. However, with an electric pencil, you can etch your initials somewhere into the frame of the bicycle in an inconspicuous place. Also etch your name or initials into the underportion of the bicycle seat. The thief can replace the seat, of course, but quite often he will not bother.

When you buy a bicycle, be sure to keep the purchase receipt. This will not only help prove ownership, but you may need it to show how much you paid for the bicycle and when you bought it in the event your insurance covers bicycle theft.

Bicycle Anti-Theft Check List

1. Just because your bicycle is in your own driveway doesn't mean it cannot be stolen. Lock the bicycle just as though you were parking it out in the street.

2. Get the best padlock and chain you can buy, or a specially made device that doesn't use a chain, such as the Kryptonite.

3. Try to avoid parking your bicycle in high-crime areas.

4. Try to avoid parking your bicycle in deserted, poorly lit areas. Overnight street parking is a sure invitation to theft.

5. Don't simply snap the lock shut when you park. Check it by pulling on it. A lock will sometimes look closed when it is not.

6. A chain and padlock are no more secure than the pole to which they are attached. If you fasten your bicycle to a wooden post, for example, it will require no great effort on the part of the thief to cut or smash through the post.

7. Make sure your bicycle is electrically marked with your initials, preferably in two places. Also be sure your name or initials are marked on the inside of the seat.

8. Keep your purchase receipt. Also memorize the name of the manufacturer of the bicycle. Be able to identify the bicycle not only by its color, but by its features as well. You should also know the bicycle model number, if it has one. You can get all this information from the descriptive catalog sheet furnished when you buy the bicycle, or it may be supplied as part of a manual. If not, then be sure to get this information from the store where you buy the bicycle. You may have to supply this information to the police and the more specific and detailed your data, the better the chances of recovery.

9. Don't lend your bicycle to friends, neighbors, or strangers without realizing that the full responsibility remains yours. You are simply lending a bicycle; that is all.

10. If you keep your bicycle parked in your garage, or in a basement, lock your bicycle just as though you were parking it out on the street. Garage doors are frequently left open and an opportunistic thief can walk in and drive out with your bicycle in a matter of seconds.

Insurance

No insurance company likes to pay out to losers, people who are regularly the victims of thieves. If you tend to be burglary prone you may find it more and more difficult to get insurance coverage or else you may suddenly realize that your premiums have skyrocketed.

Many new auto-insurance policies specifically exclude car-stereo units unless there is an extra-fee rider attached to the policy or unless the stereo is installed at the factory and thus is considered an integral part of the car.

There is confusion among claims agents on whether an in-dash installation after original sale of the auto would qualify as "factory" installation under the insurance policies. The reason the insurance companies are so tough about insuring stereo components in cars is the high incidence of car-stereo theft. If your present car stereo is covered by original equipment insurance, better check with your insurance agent if you plan to install a new radio. Your policy may not cover the new unit.

Chapter 7

Security in the Office

Like houses and apartments, cars, trailers and boats, the business office is a prime target for the burglar. In a sense, though, the office is more like a car from the burglar's point of view. A thief can look inside a car or just glance at it and he can easily see if it is occupied or not. After a certain hour, making allowance for the presence of members of a cleaning service, offices are unoccupied. Nor are they usually occupied over a weekend, particularly on Sunday, and it is fairly certain that they will be deserted during a holiday.

This doesn't mean that office thefts do not take place during normal business hours. Some thieves prefer the hours of nine to five since they can then use normal building pedestrian traffic as a cover.

At one time the prime target in an office was the office safe. But with the increased use of nighttime and weekend bank depositories that permit deposits during other than regular banking hours, the office safe has become somewhat less common. More usual targets are now office typewriters, electronic calculators, adding machines, portable duplicators, office radio and television sets.

There are some offices, though, that are of special interest to the burglar, and these include those involved in precious stones, currency exchange, silver, and other precious commodities. These offices are ordinarily more secure than the average, but are also a more tempting target.

Building Security

Many building security arrangements are pathetic. Those who man the building after office hours usually double as elevator men, superintendents, or overall caretakers. They seldom receive security training and in many cases the general attitude of the building owner is that office security is the responsibility of the individual tenant. Quite often the owners of the building use a building management service with both building service and owners primarily interested in getting an adequate return on their investment.

In many offices, visitors after hours are required to sign in and sign out. This very crude security measure is often ignored by both tenants and watchmen and, in any event, those in charge of the registration book do not know every tenant. A burglar, dressed for the part—that is, wearing a business suit and carrying a briefcase or dispatch case—and making an impressive appearance can walk with confidence to the entrance desk, sign in, and go to any floor he wishes.

In many buildings, no packages may be taken out without a pass. Passes can be made in advance by the burglar, but in many cases, the recipient of the pass, usually the head elevator operator, doesn't even bother to look at it. Since this system obviously offers such little protection, some building operators provide their own printed passes. Theoretically, only tenants are supplied with such passes, but any thief can manage to get possession of one. He can then have the pass duplicated by an offset process by any small printer. In a building having a large number of elevators and a number of different exits, such as from the front and rear, or front and side, the pass system falls apart completely. The elevator starters immediately assume that a starter on the other side of the building has asked for and received the pass.

In some buildings packages may be removed only via the freight elevator. The pass system, if in effect here, provides as little security as passes used in regular passenger elevators.

This means, then, that as far as the average office is concerned there is no perimeter protection. The burden of security then falls on the shoulder of the business office owner or his general manager.

Protecting the Office

Offices in some of the older buildings have opaque glass doors, a style that was common at one time. With a suction cup and a glass cutter, and a reasonable assurance that he is not going to be seen or disturbed, the burglar can easily cut away a section that will let him reach in and release the door lock. Most office locks are not the double-cylinder type and a key is required only for entrance. Once he has his hands inside the door, the lock is defeated and the door opens easily. The best arrangement with a glass door is to have it replaced with a metal type, with the consent and approval of the building owners or operators.

Glass doors can be, and often are, protected by a sensing-foil setup, designed to set off some kind of alarm. Sensor switches can also be used to trigger an alarm if the door is opened. The alarm can be an on-premises type, or the type that signals a warning to some externally located security agency. It is always advisable to have a sticker on the door emphasizing that the door is alarm-protected, whether or not this is actually so.

Most office locks are single-cylinder deadbolt types, and

may be more or less pick-resistant. A burglar can defeat this lock with a cylinder puller. For better protection, use a cylinder-guard plate. This will not interfere with your use of your office key and will provide greater security, making the cylinder puller useless.

The Three Steps to Office Security

There are three basic steps to office security: perimeter security, office security, and spot security. With perimeter security, the objective is to keep the burglar away from your front door. Perimeter security is a function of the building owners' operators and there is nothing much you can do about this, unless you make inquiries before you sign a building lease. Perimeter security could include adequate lighting not only in the front of the building, but of the sides and rear as well. Spotlights and floodlights are useful deterrents. Adequate perimeter security also includes a trained guard. For reasons of economy, many buildings use elderly retired persons, often retired police officers, as building guards and watchmen.

Office security means not making your office especially attractive to a burglar. In office security, it is best to keep the burglar away from the building altogether, and this is a function of perimeter security. Failing that, the next step is to discourage the burglar from entering your particular premises. You can do this by using not one, but two deadbolt-type locks having double cylinders, with a guard plate on each. You can also use an alarm system on your door. If your building is an older type and the door has a transom, nail it shut and replace the glass with solid, thick wood or metal. Make sure that your door fits snugly against the door jamb to minimize the possibility of the use of a jimmy. If your door lock is equipped with a lock alarm—and this would be helpful—also make sure that there is a decal right above it stating that the lock is so equipped.

The basic idea in perimeter and office security is to discourage the burglar from entering, by throwing obstacles in his way, and by encouraging him to think that the risk of detection is high. However, the trouble with an office is that anyone— and that means anyone—can enter during daytime working hours. A burglar, visiting an office for some contrived reason, can easily appraise the entrance and determine at a glance the possibilities of a break-in.

The office key is one of the weak links in the office-security system. The office door can be opened by building cleaners, and since this service is handled by building management, there is no way to ensure that the key will not fall into the wrong hands. Further, it is common office practice to have a number of duplicates made of the office key. The president of the business must have one, and so must the office manager. Quite often, the lowest member in the office hierarchy, the shipping clerk or the office boy, is given a key for the simple reason that they are the first to arrive and are expected to open lights, sort and deliver mail, and start the day's activities. The greater the availability of office keys and the greater their distribution, the larger the risk.

Once inside the office, the burglar can usually make away with just about anything he can carry. It is helpful to bolt all office equipment to desks—and this is done in some offices— but it can be a nuisance, particularly if the equipment is to be moved around. Some offices are now equipped with radio receivers, television sets, and may have a bar, in addition to the usual collection of general office machines. The burglar's problem is that some of the loot is bulky and heavy. Further, he has the problem of getting it out of the building undetected. And so, in many instances the theft will consist of a single item, such as a typewriter. The burglar can put this under his arm, walk down the stairs, and take the nearest building exit.

To help the police in recovering equipment, keep an inventory record of all of it, identifying each component by manufacturer, date of purchase, function, and model number. Also make a note of the serial number. You can limit the disposability of your office equipment by engraving each piece with your company name, using an electric pencil. Some offices use self-stick printed decals, but these can be removed too easily.

Unless desks contain important, private papers, they should not be locked. In forcing desk drawers a thief may do more damage than the possible loss of some paper clips and rubber bands.

Telephone Larceny

Since the office thief, working at night or over the weekend, may not be in a great hurry, he might be inclined to use your office phone to make some long-distance calls. You can prevent this by using a phone lock, but these are suitable only for dial type and not pushbutton tone phones.

Insurance

While insurance will never cover your office-equipment losses completely, it does spread the financial burden. Since insurance companies are just as interested as you are in minimizing theft, they can often supply useful information on how best to protect your office. If they have a security division, contact them and take advantage of their experience and advice. If you rent office equipment, make sure you know the extent of your liability for the equipment. At the same time, find out if your office machines are covered by insurance by the supplier, or if that is your responsibility. Similarly, if you buy office equipment on a time-purchase plan, make sure you know just what your financial responsibilities are. Ordinarily, in buying or renting office equipment the entire emphasis is on what the equipment can do. The subject of security may not even be brought up during such discussions.

Personnel

As in many department stores, theft can come from the inside as well as outside. Personnel departments screen prospective employees from a function viewpoint—that is, how well the prospective worker can do his or her job. For security, a check on background, character, and possible law violations would be helpful.

The Office Check List

The office manager is usually responsible for office security but total office security means every member of the staff must be made aware that not only the employing company, but their own personal possessions (including money) can be the target of the office thief. Here is a simple check list for making the office more secure:

1. Ask questions of any strangers in your area. If you see someone who isn't familiar, lift the phone and alert the office manager or the floor supervisor, or your immediate superior. One of the characteristics of the office thief is his disguise: He looks and acts like a business executive, and he acts bold and sure.

2. Do not allow soliciting of any kind. Most office solicitors are impervious to any rebuffs. The best way to handle them is to phone the building supervisor immediately and complain. Many office-building managements post signs forbidding the use of their premises by solicitors.

3. Keep valuables out of sight. Office machines, naturally, must be exposed. But employees, particularly female employees, should not feel that an office is positively secure. Pocketbooks should be put in desk drawers, and if possible those drawers should be locked. A pocketbook can disappear with incredible speed from the top of a desk.

4. If you have a reception area it should be kept as a closed section. This means that entry into it is by a door only and this door should be kept locked with some sort of buzzer release by the receptionist. The reception room should always have someone in it.

5. Always be sure to lock all entrance doors at the close of business. Some businesses rely on building security and use

an ordinary-type latch lock on their exit door. Replace this with a double-cylinder deadbolt lock having a security plate on the outside.

6. Keep a record of the number of keys that have been made for the main office door and make sure these are held only by responsible individuals in the company.

7. Make a record of all serial numbers of all office equipment and keep this record, plus information on date of purchase, name of supplier, and date, in an office-record vault. Also put the name of your company on all machinery with an electric pencil.

8. Warn all employees never to keep personal cash in their desk drawers.

9. The extent of your security efforts depends directly on what you want to make secure. If your office does not handle cash, has no valuable papers or equipment, and has nothing of any value for a thief, and pays its employees by individual checks, then security can be minimal. If you have a safe for bookkeeping records, put a note on the outside of the safe making such a statement.

10. Consider the possibility of having your office wired with a silent alarm to some external security agency.

Chapter 8

Travel Security

The possibility of being robbed is a form of pressure. But unlike other forms of pressure, such as job pressure or the pressure of ordinary daily living, the pressure of potential robbery with you as its victim is unrelenting and unceasing. It is this way because you never know when you will become the target. The old concept of theft by night is now a myth. Daytime robberies are now commonplace, and, as a matter of fact, the element of surprise now plays a large part in some robberies. As an example, you may be walking down the corridor of your hotel toward your room and as you reach the door a gun, seemingly from out of nowhere, will be in your back, with a disembodied voice suggesting you do nothing foolish. Within a moment, you and the thief are alone in the room, where he has an opportunity to rob you at his leisure.

This is an opportunistic type of robbery—that is, you became a victim because all the circumstances were right. You were alone, there was no one else in the corridor, and you were about to open the door to your room; at least one of your hands was occupied, making you defenseless to that extent, and you may have had a purse or package in the other hand. Preventing this type of robbery is almost impossible unless you can always make an arrangement to have someone with you at all times.

However, if there is no alternative to robbery, you can at least plan ahead to minimize its effects. One method is never to carry any more cash with you than is absolutely essential. If you must carry money, try to arrange to have as much of it as possible in travelers' checks. They are low in cost, readily obtainable in banks, and you can get a refund if you are robbed. Of course, you should keep some currency in your wallet or purse, but this should not be more than necessary to cover daily requirements.

For some individuals, however, cash in a wallet or purse is a form of psychological security blanket. Such persons do not feel comfortable unless they have some assurance that they can reach cash and touch it in a matter of moments. The alternative is to carry a money belt (for the men) and a money pouch (for either men or women). The money belt looks like the usual sort of belt, but has a compartment in which a small amount of bills can be cached. The money pouch looks something like a belt, but can be used to carry a larger sum. Unlike the belt it is worn beneath the clothing and, aside from some minor discomfort, is a good money-security measure.

For the men, a wallet having a hidden money compartment is also available and this can be used to secrete cash. There is always the possibility that the thief will take the wallet as well as its contents, but then again he may not and so you have at least some chance that you will not lose all your money. In some cases, the thief may compel his victims to strip, and so the presence of the money pouch will immediately become evident. But he may not require this action and so the use of the money pouch will also keep the loss from becoming total.

The sum and substance of all this is that you have no guarantee. The behavior of a thief is unpredictable. Some will resort to violence if they feel that their time and efforts have not been adequately rewarded. A thief who needs fifty dollars for a fix will not willingly settle for ten. He is well aware that a second robbery for the additional money he must have will not only take time but will increase his risk proportionately.

Aside from the money belt, the money pouch, and travelers' checks, there are a few more precautions you can take. Avoid the habit of carrying large bills. Ten-dollar denominations are much better than twenties and twenties are certainly better than fifty- or hundred-dollar bills. The sight of a large roll of bills can attract attention. In that case the thief will follow you until you give him the opportunity to make his move in relative safety.

To avoid making an ostentatious show of money, you might try keeping most of your cash in a money belt or pouch, but if these don't appeal to you, you might consider the two-wallet technique. With this method you keep most of your money in one wallet, with that wallet carefully secured in an inside pocket (never a hip pocket). This wallet should be zippered into position and the pocket should be deep enough to cover the wallet completely. You can then keep your spare currency, enough to cover your daily needs, in the other wallet.

Many thieves prefer women as targets of opportunity for a number of reasons. One of these is that it takes a woman much longer to reach into her pocketbook for her money purse than it does for a man to reach for his wallet. A man can have his wallet out and back again in a fraction of the time it usually takes a woman to fish around in her pocketbook for her purse, thus giving the thief a longer opportunity to snatch the purse.

There is also a big difference, possibly psychological, in the way men and women pay their bills. If people are lined up ready to pay a cashier, most of the men will have their money in their hands before reaching the cashier. A woman will usually wait until she is directly in front of the cashier before opening her purse. A thief, aware of these male-female differences, cannot predict when a man will take out his wallet. All he knows is that it will be sometime while he is waiting in line. But, under some pretense or other, he can wait directly in the vicinity of the cashier, and assess rather well just how much cash a woman has available.

Another reason a thief may prefer a woman as a target, other than the obvious one that the woman is usually weaker, is that a woman's purse may be much more accessible than a man's wallet. The woman's purse is in her pocketbook, but that pocketbook is external to the woman's clothing. It is easier to jostle, to move it, and to do things with it. A man's wallet isn't external to the man's clothing, but is actually imbedded in layers of it. This doesn't mean a man's wallet cannot be removed without detection. It happens regularly, but it does require the effort of a professional. For the amateur—and there are many more of those than there are professionals—the woman's pocketbook is a more tempting and more available target of opportunity.

There is still one more reason why women are becoming more likely victims and the fault—if blame is to be assigned— lies with the men. In many marriages women not only work as housekeepers and mothers but also perform the functions of a treasurer. In many households a wife is expected to balance the budget, handle all finances, maintain the checking account in proper shape, and to pay during a shopping expedition. This means she carries the money—not all of it, but quite often most of it, particularly if the couple are traveling. All the more reason, then, for the woman to become the victim.

Eyeball-to-Eyeball Confrontation

For the victim a robbery can be, and often is, a traumatic experience. But, aside from the fact that a robbery is the involuntary transfer of some of your wealth to a stranger, a robbery in which the victim and the thief are fairly close to each other is a form of communication—not a pleasant form, but communication nevertheless.

To the thief, the victim is nameless and faceless, not a human being, but an object barring the way to the money he wants. If he resorts to violence, he will do so because he isn't taking action against another human being. But you can become more than just an object if you look into the eyes of the thief. This eyeball-to-eyeball confrontation is a form of communication in which your relationship, not as thief and victim, but as a pair of human beings, is established. When this happens, the thief is less likely to resort to violence. It doesn't mean the robbery will stop, but it does mean there is less likelihood you will be hurt. Yes, there are exceptions, as there are to almost everything else. Many victims are so terrified that they concentrate on the weapon instead of the person holding it. Of course, it is easy to give advice, and it is certainly more difficult to remember what to do to prevent a robbery and how to act during one, but at least you will have been forewarned, and that may help.

Judo and Karate

Judo and karate are two of the more common forms of self-defense. Many individuals take courses in these activities as protection in case of attack. There is nothing wrong with that, but generally these efforts are undertaken in a burst of enthusiasm that dies out after two or three lessons. A small number of lessons will not only not make you an expert, but may give you a wholly unwarranted feeling of self-confidence. It takes a lot of effort, self-discipline, and continuous practice to become a judo or karate expert, and if you have done this, then you are indeed in a position to repel an attack. A determined thief with a knife, gun, or other potentially lethal weapon is usually more than a match for a beginner in judo. Practice judo before you are robbed, not during.

Hotel Theft

You can be robbed in your hotel room even though you have the door locked. Since the same key to a hotel (or motel) room is used by so many people—including the fact that there is always a master key around somewhere—it shouldn't be too surprising that having a duplicate key made is no great problem.

Your hotel or motel room, then, is not safe while you are away simply because keys are so readily accessible. The room may be safe if you do more than just close the door. Such rooms are generally equipped with deadlocks that can be adjusted only from inside the room. Don't assume you will close the deadlatch at the time you retire. You may or may not. Lock the deadlatch as soon as you close the door. In that way you will be sure to avoid unwelcome visitors.

A special traveler's lock is available if you want hotel- or motel-room protection while you are away. This doesn't mean the thief can't overcome the lock. He may be able to do so with enough time, but generally the sight of such a lock is enough to encourage him to move along to a door that doesn't present such problems. After all, there are numerous rooms available and there is no reason why he should spend an unnecessary amount of time on one that poses a problem.

If you have valuables with you in a hotel or motel room, it may be better to deposit these in a safe-deposit box provided by the management. You should also learn of the extent of responsibility for theft assumed by the management. And, you should also have traveler's insurance on all valuable items you carry with you. Check with your insurance agent on the extent of your responsibility—that is, whether you are required by your policy to store your valuables in a hotel safe during night hours.

Losing Your Luggage

The suitcases you carry aren't made for you alone, even though you may have personally selected them for their style, shape, and color. First, make sure that the luggage you buy comes equipped with at least one lock, preferably two. Make sure these are locked, not simply closed shut, when you travel. Attach a name tag to each piece of luggage, so that if you and the luggage become separated, there is a chance the finder of the luggage will find you also.

But this isn't enough. Put a self-stick strip of colored plastic across some prominent area of your luggage. This will immediately identify it as yours. It will make it much easier for you to locate your luggage when it is mixed in with a large number of other pieces of luggage, and it allows for easier identification if your luggage should happen to stray. If your luggage does become lost, complain immediately to the transportation service: bus, cab, train, ship, or plane. Most transportation companies assume very limited liability for luggage and its contents. Depending on what you carry it may (or may not) be worthwhile for you to carry supplementary insurance.

If you must turn your luggage over to someone else, as in the case of a plane, be sure to get a baggage receipt and do not release this receipt except in exchange for your luggage. This receipt will not only document the luggage as yours, but fixes responsibility on the carrier, and should help in the location of your luggage, assuming, of course, that it hasn't been stolen.

Your Credit Cards

Most persons who travel keep their credit cards in the same wallet with their cash. Don't. Get a separate carrying case for your credit cards and put them in an inside pocket that is well-secured and deep. Somewhere, keep a record of your credit-card numbers and the name of the issuing credit-card organization. Notify them immediately if your credit cards are stolen. Never, under any circumstances, lend your credit cards to anyone else, and that includes relatives. Do not allow credit cards out of your possession, except for the few moments you need for paying a bill. Then, be sure to remember to get your credit card back. Quite commonly, a man or woman, most conscientious with cash, will walk away after making a purchase, with the credit card in the possession of the cashier.

Do not flash your credit cards any more than you would with money. In many ways a credit card is more valuable than money for it is actually an invitation to unlimited spending. Your credit card has provision for your signature. Sign it. That signature may be some help in preventing the use of the card in the event it is stolen.

The best credit card is one that has your photograph as an additional form of identification. Unfortunately, many persons receiving credit cards in payment for bills fail to make the necessary check between the person holding the credit card and the picture.

Car Pooling

After leaving an airport, or a train terminal, it is tempting to share a cab, particularly if a taxi is difficult to get, and especially if the weather is rather bad. You may be asked to become a communal cab passenger by someone you just met on the train or plane, or it might be someone at the taxi station. Consider, however, that a taxi is quite unlike a subway, trolley, or bus. The taxi driver and the other passenger may form part of a holdup team. You can easily be separated from your wallet and your luggage and then unceremoniously dumped in a strange part of the city.

There are two basic types of taxis. One is operated by a reputable business organization; the other is known as a gypsy cab. The gypsy is an independently owned cab, and may not be registered with the city authorities. And it may simply be cruising in an effort to get some "easy pickings." This doesn't mean that all gypsy cabs are operated by thieves, and that all cab drivers of registered taxis are shiningly honest. The odds, though, are not in favor of the gypsy. If you plan to use a taxi you'll find it helpful to be able to distinguish between the gypsy and other cabs. Spend a few minutes looking at the taxicab traffic and you'll soon get to know which is which. A bus or trolley may take longer, but it is safer. And so is an airport bus.

Watching Your Luggage

The best thing you can do for your luggage is to keep an eye on it. As soon as the luggage is returned to you by your transportation service, you are once again fully responsible. Never leave your luggage unattended. Thus, putting your luggage outside a men's or ladies' room while you go inside for just a few minutes is inviting theft. And don't ask strangers to keep an eye on your luggage for you while you go off to make a phone call. The stranger may do more than you have asked. If you do make a phone call, squeeze the luggage inside the phone booth with you, even if it means you will be somewhat crowded. In the brief moment you may turn your head aside while inside the booth your luggage, carefully placed outside, can literally vanish.

Small-change thieves—those who are satisfied to make just a few dollars—often make railway, plane, and bus terminals their places of business. They seem to favor bus lines, though. Do not use the services of anyone offering to act as a porter, even though the offer may come from a young, pleasant-looking boy who is apparently just trying to make an honest dollar. He may be young—many bus-terminal thieves are—but honest he is not. Keep a strong grip on your bags and surrender them only to a bona-fide porter. He will be wearing a uniform and his cap will probably have the word "porter" written on it.

But no matter who carries your bags, do not let them out of your sight. Bags can not only be stolen, but they can become lost or strayed. Tracing your luggage can be time-consuming, aggravating, and extremely inconvenient. When paying for luggage-handling service, don't reach in for your wallet. Keep enough loose change in your pants pocket to pay for this service. This will enable you to pay without revealing the location and contents of your wallet.

Sleeping and Theft

During a trip, whether by bus, train, or plane, the motion of the vehicle, plus the fatigue produced by traveling, often induces sleep. Again, this is an open invitation to theft. The person sitting next to you, with the help of a garment such as a coat, or a newspaper if the weather is warm, can easily open a pocketbook completely undetected. Further, you will not know of the theft until sometime after it has happened, and while you may suspect that the person sitting adjacent to you was responsible, you will never be sure.

The best place to sit is immediately adjacent to a window, and not an aisle seat. With a window seat you can put your pocketbook between yourself and the window, putting the thief in a position of having to reach across you. This doesn't mean he can't do so, but at least you have put an obstacle in his way. Do not put the pocketbook into its position by itself. Keep your arm through the straps, and give the pocketbook one twist so that the straps do exert some slight pressure on your arm. Then put a garment, such as a sweater or coat, over the pocketbook so that it just doesn't sit there as a direct temptation. The trouble with an aisle seat is that you must either keep the pocketbook on your lap, or between yourself and an adjacent stranger. Your lap is the better location, but again, give the pocketbook one turn to twist the straps and then cover it with a garment. Naturally, if you are carrying cash or valuables you do not want to lose, avoid opening your pocketbook. If you need chewing gum, lipstick, a mirror, or whatnot, take these items along in a small carryall designed just for that purpose.

If you are being met at a terminal by someone who is a complete stranger, get a description before you make the trip. As a further check, ask a few leading questions that will help make the identification a positive one.

Check List for Traveling Security

The unfortunate part about security is that it requires unending vigilance. For maximum protection you must exercise constant alertness and awareness so that you may not become a victim. It is unfortunate since it requires you to be suspicious of people who may very well be honest and interesting companions and who, possibly like yourself, are reaching out for human contact without the slightest thought of possible gain. It also means that instead of concentrating completely on your business or your travel plans, you must devote some time to an activity that, by its very nature, puts a sort of wall around you. The alternative, though, from a viewpoint of financial loss, physical harm, and shock, is a very high price to pay.

Before you go on a trip, consider what precautions you should take before leaving and during the trip.

1. Make a record of your credit-card numbers. Keep a list of them in a small pocket notebook so that you can supply these numbers to the issuing credit organization without delay. Your personal liability, or its extent, may depend on how quickly you do this. And, before you leave, supply a duplicate record of the credit-card numbers to your office secretary or your wife or to someone else who is equally dependable. Thus, if your credit cards are lost or stolen, and if your own personal notebook record disappears at the same time, you can get the information you need just by making a telephone call.

Never let your credit cards out of your possession for any longer than it takes a cashier or sales clerk to make up your purchase slip. And, when doing this, do not let yourself be diverted by conversation, or by thinking about your travel plans. Get your credit card back and make sure it is in a separate wallet, placed in a hard-to-get-at, deep inner pocket.

2. Before you leave, make a realistic estimate of the amount of cash you will need to take with you. If your travels include visiting a particular town or city on a regular basis, consider the advantage of opening an account at a bank in that city, preferably located near your hotel. In this way you will be able to reduce the amount of money you feel you must have with you.

Your currency should have the smallest, convenient denomination. Flashing a hundred-dollar bill for a five-dollar purchase may be impressive and it is, for it will undoubtedly attract attention. The two-wallet idea is a nuisance but it is a helpful security measure. Keep your credit cards and travelers' checks in one and your currency in another. For your currency wallet, select a wallet that permits the currency to be flat at all times, thus producing a less noticeable bulge in your jacket. Your clothing will look better for it. Never put your wallet in a back hip pocket. It is very convenient to keep currency in pants pocket, held together with a money clip. But this means you can lose it to the first skillful pickpocket who comes along.

3. If you carry a briefcase attach an identification card to the handle with your name, address, and phone number clearly printed. Put a similar identification inside the briefcase. If the briefcase is to contain valuable, confidential papers, make sure it can be locked. Keep it locked, even if it is to be placed next to your seat in a plane or train. The same sort of thinking applies to an attaché case. To avoid the nuisance of keeping and using a key, consider briefcases and attaché cases that use combination locks. These can generally be set to any number you indicate. Select a number that has meaning for you, so you won't forget it. If, for example, your birthday is January 25, then you can make the lock combination 125 (with the digit 1 representing the first month of the year). The vendor from whom you buy your briefcase or attaché case can set the combination to any three-digit number you select.

Many briefcases and attaché cases look somewhat alike. As a quick aid to identification, have your initials affixed. If you have a choice of initial styles, just make sure they are sufficiently large so that they can be read easily, and that they are legible. Some initials, made in an Old English font, are quite attractive, but are also almost impossible to read.

Do not carry more confidential business information in your attaché or briefcase than you absolutely require. The best place for such papers is in a safe.

4. If you use limousine or bus service and your baggage is to be loaded, generally into a side compartment in the bus, or the rear of a limousine, make sure that your luggage is loaded. Do not take your bus or limousine seat until it is. If your luggage is equipped with identification stripes in color,

it will be easy to recognize. If your luggage remains on the sidewalk when your bus or limousine pulls away, you will be quite fortunate if you see it again.

Do not give in to suggestions from any bus or limousine driver that your luggage will follow on a subsequent car. It may, or it may not. If for some reason your luggage must remain to wait for the next available vehicle, wait with it.

5. If, during traveling, you make the casual acquaintance of someone sitting next to you, do not reveal anything of your traveling plans, or the name of your hotel. The queries you get may be innocent, but then again, they may not be.

6. If, as part of your travel plans, you rent a car, treat it as though it were your own and exercise the same precautions you do at home. Don't park on a dark street or a street that isn't adequately lighted. If possible, park in an inside garage, even if there is street parking space available. Do not leave anything more than the ignition key with the parking attendant.

Obviously, it isn't always possible to follow these suggestions. If you must park on a dark street, don't rush to the car on your return. First, look to see if no one is lurking about. A car thief will sometimes wait for the return of the car owner or operator, and will then not only steal the car, but rob the owner or operator as well.

Again, if your rented car is parked on a dark street, have the door key (this is usually the ignition key as well) out and ready to use. You should be able to walk up to the car and open the door immediately, without fumbling around in your pockets. Do not remain at that spot for any longer than absolutely necessary. Drive away at once, and then, if you must examine some papers or stop for any other reason, select a well-lighted area, preferably one with ample street traffic.

The situation is much more difficult for women. A woman is likely to put up less of a defense than a man and so is a more attractive target. Further, as mentioned earlier, women have a habit of waiting until the last possible moment before opening a pocketbook. Remove your car keys from your pocketbook and have your door key ready long before you walk down a dark, deserted street to your car. And drive away as quickly as you can. If possible, try to arrange for an escort to your car.

7. Don't pick up hitchhikers under any circumstances, not even if the hitchhiker is a woman carrying a baby in her arms. This ploy has actually been used. Any male hitchhiker is a potential thief and a potential murderer. Police files are filled with records of kindly drivers who ended up robbed and killed.

Don't stop your car to ask directions of pedestrians. And be suspicious of such an answer as "I'm heading that way myself. Let me go along with you and I'll show you exactly where it is." Instead, drive into the nearest service station. They get requests for directions quite often and are usually familiar with the various roads.

8. Don't start out with a road map and fond hopes that you will arrive at your destination in due course. Instead, plan your trip so that you avoid getting to your destination late at night, particularly if you must drive through or stop in some high-crime area. If for any reason you are menaced while you are in your car, turn on your emergency flashing lights, and keep beeping your horn. Don't lean on the horn so it emits a steady blast. Most people will think your horn is stuck. A series of horn blasts will attract the kind of attention you want.

9. When you get to your hotel or motel, put all valuables you do not require in the hotel or motel safe. This doesn't mean the safe cannot be robbed. And it doesn't mean that the hotel or motel proprietors assume full responsibility for your valuables. It does mean that your property is more protected in a safe than in a motel or hotel room. Ask for safe privileges when you check in and deposit your property at once. Don't wait until you get to your room. However, if this isn't possible or practical for you, do so as soon as you can after you are in your room. If a bellboy accompanies you to your room, ask him to wait a minute or two to accompany you down to the safe-deposit area.

If you do have valuables, don't try to hide them in your hotel or motel room. First, there aren't that many available hiding places and second, you can be sure that any experienced burglar knows where to look—certainly much better than you do. Do not leave your wallet or jewelry on a dresser or bed where it can be seen, and don't imagine your possessions will be safe just because you store them in your luggage, even if you lock the luggage. Luggage locks will not stop a professional thief. They are easy to open and all they can do is to ensure that your luggage will remain closed in transportation and to discourage the inexperienced, opportunistic thief.

10. Your first step in a hotel or motel room should be to inspect the lock on the door and to make sure you understand fully how it works. When you are in your room, don't assume you are safe just because the door is closed. Most rooms are now equipped with deadbolt locks that can be operated from the inside only. Your first action in the room should be to close the deadlock. You will also probably find a lock with a chain permitting you to open the door a few inches, but with the chain preventing forcible entry. When answering the door, make sure this chain lock is in position before you open the door. If you have any doubt about the person on the other side of your door, telephone the desk clerk. Don't open the door for people who claim to be plumbers, television-set repairmen, or package-delivery messengers. Have them wait while you telephone the desk clerk for confirmation. Don't ever let yourself be panicked by someone at your door claiming to have an urgent message for you requiring your immediate attention or signature.

11. If, upon return to your motel or hotel, you see someone acting suspiciously in front of your door, or if there are one or two men who seem to be working on it, return at once to the main floor and report your suspicions to the desk clerk.

Do not use stairways in a hotel unless you go up and down with a group. Use operator-type elevators in preference to self-service types. Try to avoid going into an elevator alone. If necessary, wait for a group.

When you register in a hotel, be sure to ask for a room on a lower floor, such as the second or third. Thus, when getting into an elevator, first making certain it is occupied by other people, you have an assurance they will at least accompany you in the elevator as far as your floor. If, for example your room is on or near the top floor, it is quite likely you will be alone for at least the last few floors. Hotel thieves are aware of this and so take an "up" elevator for the last few floors, hoping to find a victim alone in an elevator.

11. Before going away from your room, try the door to make sure it is locked. Don't assume this is so just because you closed the door. Try the doorknob and twist it to make sure the door is really locked. When leaving your room, don't turn off all the lights. You should have one or two lamps turned on so that the room is fully illuminated. A thief can walk down a hotel or motel corridor, and just by looking at the bottom of the door can get an idea if the room is occupied. A complete absence of light indicates that the occupants are either out or are sleeping. If you have a travel lock with you, and you should, make sure it is inserted in the door properly by following the manufacturer's instructions.

If, upon your return, you find your door open, do not enter the room. Instead, go to the main desk and notify the desk clerk. Your room may be occupied by a cleaner, but then again it may not. A well-organized hotel or motel knows where its cleaners are at all times. And don't feel embarrassed if the door to your room is open for some perfectly legitimate reason. It is much better to be embarrassed than to be robbed.

12. If you are in a town or city that is new to you either check with friends or with the hotel or motel management about safe areas and areas to avoid. In some sections it may not be wise to walk on the streets after dark, or during the early evening.

Even if you receive assurances that you will be absolutely safe on the streets at all times, stay out of alleys, no matter how quaint or historic they may seem to be. Don't take a shortcut, if that shortcut means you must walk across a vacant lot that isn't lighted. When walking down a street, stay on the pavement alongside the curb to avoid being pulled into a doorway or hall.

If, when walking down a street, you see an individual or

a group approaching on your side and you sense the possibility of trouble, walk to the other side of the street. If you must walk down a dimly lit street, use the roadway normally reserved for cars and try to walk in a direction opposite that of traffic. In this way you will be able to see oncoming cars.

13. If you walk past a parked car and someone calls to you from it, ignore the call and any remarks that may be made. And if, while you are walking, someone stops in front of you and asks for a match or wants to know the time, don't stop. Just keep on moving. If you hear any strange noises coming from a car, from a side street, from inside a house or building, pay no attention. These are all devices used for stopping pedestrians and maneuvering them into a position or area where they can be robbed, assaulted, or both.

14. If you are held up, consider that your life is worth far more than your money or jewelry. The average person is no match for a man with a knife or gun, particularly if the holder of the knife or gun is high on drugs, has a resentment against society, or is sadistically inclined. An experienced person might be able to appraise the thief quite well, but the majority of persons cannot. Thieves, particularly those that specialize in hotel rooms, usually work in pairs. If you are held up by a pair on the street or in your hotel room, you are not only outweaponed but outnumbered as well.

15. Some hotels and motels are now posting warning signs, alerting their customers against specific types of theft that have become common. Read these signs and follow their instructions carefully. They are based on experience.

This does not mean that if you follow all these suggestions you will be absolutely safe on a trip. It does mean that you get more favorable odds. There are very few deterrents you can use when on a trip. At home you may have an alarm system or a dog, or you may have heavy deadbolt locks. Also, at home you know which are the relatively safe areas and you recognize which are the areas to avoid. You don't have this advantage in a strange city. You are also at a disadvantage if the section in which you live has a very low crime rate. This may make you careless about personal security and it may make you somewhat more trusting of people than you should be.

Being robbed while you are on a trip means more than the loss of money or possessions. The shock may make you incapable of conducting your business. If you are on a pleasure trip, your initial reaction will be to cancel the trip and get home as quickly as possible. It will also make you hesitate about taking other such trips. And so a robbery can affect you in many ways.

We cannot emphasize often enough that one of the biggest problems for the average individual is acquiring security-consciousness, and that too many of us have an "it can't happen to me" attitude. However, with an increasing crime rate, the chances are that it will happen to you. Why become a statistic?

Chapter 9

Miscellaneous Security Information

The growth of the crime rate has set the pace for a parallel growth in devices to combat crime. Combat is an unfortunate choice of word, for it implies that the law-abiding citizen and the maufacturers of security equipment aggressively seek out criminals in an effort to eliminate them. That may be true for a police department, and even then not for the entire police force, but it is not true of the citizen. It is the thief who is active and aggressive, while the average person protects himself only passively. There are some who carry guns, either licensed by the police or acting independently, who repel criminal activities with a show of force. A criminal has an option. He can use force, or not, as he wishes. A citizen, though, is not in a position to counter force with force, for a number of reasons. Unlike the criminal, a law-abiding citizen isn't force oriented. He doesn't think or act in terms of force, and never has occasion to use it. He may not be permitted to carry a gun, for which a license is often required, nor is he accustomed to the use of a gun.

Finally, the criminal is protected by law in the amount of force you may use against him. You may, for example, be held up in the street by someone who looks to be about twenty, but who is later shown to be only fifteen, with what appears to be a gun, but which subsequently exhibited in court as a poorly made toy imitation. If your response to the attempted holdup is violence on your part that sends the young thief to the hospital, you may very well be in more legal trouble than your assailant.

There is no way in which a citizen knows what he should or should not do. In many states you are under an obligation to avoid violence if you possibly can. And you must show that you tried to retreat, that you did not seek the encounter, but that you did everything you reasonably could to avoid it. You may even be put in a position of attempting to convince a jury that the force you used in protecting yourself during a holdup was reasonable. And if, in a courtroom, the attorney for the thief can claim that you overreacted, then you may find yourself in more trouble than if you had simply handed over your wallet and other possessions at once.

This doesn't mean that if someone strikes at you with a knife that all you can do is utter a verbal protest. However, keep in mind that if you succeed in overcoming the criminal by the use of force, you may be put in the position of having to prove that your defense was justifiable. Thus, if you and your wife are subjected to a string of obscenities, and you react with some sort of physical attack, you may very well find yourself the defendant in a law case.

If this sounds unfair to you, if you feel that our criminals are coddled and overprotected, the answer is not to blame the police. They simply enforce the laws enacted by legislators whom you elect. In may cases the police do excellent work in bringing criminals in to court, only to find that the criminal is given a sentence in no way commensurate with his crime, and often released so quickly that he is encouraged to continue a life of crime. What is happening is the result of a permissive society. To change it you must let your legislators know, and know emphatically, that you not only want change but that you insist on it. When legislators finally pass laws that protect the citizen rather than the criminal, it will only be because you demanded it—not as a favor, but as your right. And make no mistake about it. You have a right to be secure in the street, in a bus, train, or plane, in a railroad or airplane terminal, in a motel or hotel, in your home, or in your automobile.

The thief is not a taxpayer. You are. Everything you see around you is paid for by your work and that not only includes your home, but the streets you walk on or the highways you ride on.

Self-Protection

We now have an enormous self-defense industry and there are so many devices, gadgets, and gimmicks you can use that it is almost impossible to describe them except in general terms. Some of the defense measures do not fall into any particular category, and so do not logically fit into any of the preceding chapters.

A mugging is somewhat different from an ordinary holdup. A mugging involves physical contact between the thief and the victim. Instead of threatening force, the mugger uses it at once. A mugging is generally carried out by two or more individuals, although there are some muggers who are loners.

In a two-man mugging, one of the attackers comes up from behind and puts his arm around the victim's throat, exerting considerable pressure. With this kind of attack, the victim's natural response is to put both his hands against the arm that is choking him. During this time he is being frisked by the second attacker who doesn't ask where the wallet is, but goes right ahead looking for it, removing jewelry and rings at the same time.

A mugger can render his victim unconscious in a matter of seconds. Since the mugger is accustomed to violence and uses it as part of his operation, any reaction on the part of the victim other than absolute submission is countered by still more violence. Quite often the mugger will end the robbery with violence against the victim that is neither logical nor justified. There is no way to predict the behavior of a mugger, particularly if he is an addict.

There are certain circumstances in which you may find it advisable to fight back. The first, of course, is that you must be in reasonably good physical condition. There is no point in repelling a thief successfully if the price you pay is a heart attack. But if you are attacked by someone not using a knife or gun or a lead pipe—that is, if the thief believes he can take you using just his fists—and if you are physically capable of countering, then the first thing you should do is to keep from being attacked from behind. If possible, move your back against a wall. And don't keep the fight a nice, quiet affair. That is just what your attacker wants. Scream, yell, make as much noise as you can. This will have two effects, both helpful. The first is that it will disconcert your attacker, and second, it will make him apprehensive that the racket you are making will bring help.

Remember also that you may be fighting for your life, so this is no time to be Mr. Nice Guy. Kick and kick violently. Aim for the shinbone. If your assailant is wearing a topcoat or over-coat, a kick in the groin may not hurt, particularly if you are inexperienced in making this kind of kick. But no matter what kind of coat the thief is wearing, it doesn't cover the region right above the ankles.

If you've had just one or two lessons in judo or karate, forget it. Just strike out with your hands and feet, trying to inflict the maximum amount of physical damage.

The Sex Criminal

Just as there are various kinds of burglars, so too do we have various kinds of sex criminals. Some are men who simply expose themselves to women and often to female children.

They usually select a time, place, and victim so as not to be readily apprehended. The usual claim made for exhibitionists is that they are sick, and should be treated as such, rather than as criminals. Granted. But they should not be out on the streets. They should not be out in society but in a hospital, preferably one associated with a prison.

In a crime of this kind—and it is a crime, no matter what other name may be given to it by sociologists and psychologists —little or no attention is paid to the victim, possibly because the victim has lost nothing of physical value, no money nor jewelry. But the experience can be traumatic, and can inflict emotional damage, possibly lasting a lifetime.

The most passive type of sex criminal is the voyeur, or Peeping Tom. He likes to watch women undress. The cure is not to give him an opportunity. However, against this consider that, generally speaking, women are exhibitionists and men are voyeurs. Men like to see women undress and women enjoy being watched. If a man, often accompanied by his wife, attends a night club he may get vicarious satisfaction out of what he sees on the stage. No criminal act is committed. The stage performers know what they are expected to do and often regard themselves as artists. There is no violence, no intrusion into someone else's privacy or life, no traumatic shock. The Peeping Tom, however, is intruding on someone else's privacy, and while he may do no outward physical damage, can be responsible for emotional shock on the part of his victim if he is discovered. Like the exhibitionist, the voyeur may be in urgent need of psychological treatment.

Of all sex criminals, the rapist is the most dangerous. He is the most dangerous, not only because of the rape itself, with the attendant possibilities of pregnancy and disease, but because he may very well terminate the rape with murder.

There is a common misconception that a woman who submits without fuss to a rapist is immune to violence. Violence is such a common accompaniment to rape that a victim can logically expect to be killed. It is the unharmed victim that is the exception, not the rule.

For a woman alone in a room, the best protection is a deadbolt lock and a chain guard that requires a key. A telephone also provides security. And, of course, in this one respect a woman must be more security-conscious than a man, for the simple reason that she is more vulnerable.

The potential rapist is also aware that the law is on his side and not that of the victim. He can always claim that he was enticed, seduced, that the woman willingly opened her door and invited him in, or that she offered herself in exchange for money. The rapist also knows that many women are too ashamed to report a rape, and do not want the humiliation of the act known to their friends or their husbands. She is also aware that her story of being raped may not be believed.

Since violence on the part of the rapist is almost inevitable, a woman should do everything within her power to discourage the rape. When approached she should scream, yell, kick, and create the maximum disturbance. If possible, she should pick up a heavy object and throw it, not at the rapist, but right through the window.

The rapist may be equipped with a knife or gun, and may threaten to use these weapons. True. But the odds are very likely that he will use them anyway on a submissive female. The best action in the case of potential rape is to do everything possible to forestall it.

Body Alarm System

An alarm system in the home or office is a good crime deterrent in the sense that it will stop many—not all—burglars from continuing their efforts. It all depends on the burglar, his experience with alarm systems, his ability to discontinue and defeat the alarm quickly, and also on the sophistication of the system you have had installed. Thus, an alarm that has a horn both inside and outside the house is better than one that is just an in-house type. A system that turns on house lights at the same time it triggers the alarm is more effective than one that just operates the alarm.

You can also carry an alarm system with you. For women,

the alarm looks like a small pocketbook and is equipped with shoulder straps similar to those used with ladies' handbags. For men the alarm is strapped on by a belt. The alarm (Rembrandt Security Systems, Inc.) can be used when you are a pedestrian, or you can put it on your car seat, or take it with you into a hotel or motel room. The unit is a solid-state device and is battery powered. Various types of cases are supplied, one of which looks like a typical carryall for photographic equipment.

Using a Gun

It would seem that a gun would be a logical deterrent and should be included along with door and window locks, and alarm systems. And yet a gun has such serious limitations that you can get substantial arguments pro and con about its use. Many police departments (not all) are adamantly opposed to the in-house use of a gun, warning that the average individual is really not fully aware of the responsibility involved in owning a gun.

Today, the entire emphasis is on crime prevention through the use of deterrent devices. By following perimeter, area, and point protection you can have reasonable assurance of security. But unlike door and window locks, or an alarm system, a gun is intended for use in a confrontation. Alarms and window and door locks, though, are passive devices. They do not attack. A gun in the hands of a usually law-abiding citizen is not only a deterrent but a means of punishment. Under the stress of a robbery, it is possible to use more than reasonable force, and some courts, taking into consideration the age of the thief, might punish the gun user more than the burglar.

The problem with a gun is that many people just don't know how to handle one. According to the National Safety Council, about thirteen hundred people are accidentally killed by guns each year—not out in the street, or in a holdup, but in their own homes with their own guns. And this does not include all those who are wounded by such weapons.

However, if you feel a gun is your best protection, the first thing to do is to find out if you are permitted by law in your area to have a gun. Visit your local police department and discuss the matter with them. If a permit is required, make sure you get one (assuming it will be issued to you) before buying a gun. Get the advice of the police department on what kind of gun to purchase, how often to practice, and where you may practice. Don't practice by yourself in some remote wooded area. You may hurt some other person or animal. Try pistol practice only if it is supervised.

Just one final word about guns. The burglar who invades your premises may or may not have a gun. If he is a professional, you can be sure he will have his exit planned before he touches so much as a single item in your home. He is not a belligerent and is seldom armed. He is aware that the penalty for burglary with a weapon, such as a gun, can add many years to his prison sentence if he is caught.

The second type of home burglar, now the most common type, is the youthful offender. He may be armed. He may carry a gun, or a knife, or both. Unlike the professional, he probably doesn't have his exit planned. The best thing, if you want to avoid violence, is to give him every opportunity to escape. If you corner him, he will fight, and then there is a question of whether you or he will survive a gun battle. He may very well win since he is probably more accustomed to handling a gun than the average person. Other than professionals, such as various members of a police department or security guards, most people do not take the time for gun practice once they have learned the basic rules for handling the weapon and have fired it a few times.

The third type of home burglar is the addict, and there is no way in which you can know what he is going to do. As a general rule, the addict isn't violent (yes, there are exceptions) and is only interested in earning enough for his next fix.

You should also realize that if you have a gun you must make sure it is out of the reach of the other members of your family, particularly your children. Consider also that during a burglary you may not have time enough to get to your gun and that any attempt on your part to do so could provoke a violent reaction.

All of this sounds anti-gun, but it isn't intended to be that way. A gun is dangerous. The whole point is whether you will be qualified to accept its responsibility.

Installing a Home-Protection System

Many home owners are quite handy, and have a fairly good working knowledge of tools, electricity, and wiring. If you are one of these there is no reason why you cannot install your own home alarm system. The advantage of doing so is that by installing your own you will have the confidence to wire in all the windows and doors, instead of just one or two. Further, you will feel able to make any modifications or additions, gradually updating your alarm system from an elementary type to one that is quite sophisticated. Also, you will be able to make repairs at once should such repairs become necessary.

Having a system installed is more expensive since the cost of labor is quite often more than the cost of the materials. The advantage, of course, is the convenience of having someone do the job for you—someone who has all the necessary tools, knows from experience just where to mount the alarm, and can give you substantial advice on just which areas of entry should be protected.

Places of Entry

The place of entry by a burglar into a home does vary. But data submitted by 1,941 city police departments throughout the United States during October, 1961, to the FBI, showed that doors were a more frequent place of entry for residential burglaries than for nonresidential burglaries.

There are a number of good reasons why a burglar will select a door as his entry (and his exit) area. It may be habit. We are more accustomed to going in and out of doors than through windows. Further the entry through a window may not be convenient—that is, the window may be too far above the ground. Finally, the burglar knows that if his robbery is successful, his arms may be loaded with your household goods. He wants to be able to get out with as much as he can and so a door is the logical exit.

This means, then, that in a security setup on the home, the front door requires the most attention. This is particularly true in apartment houses, where windows may not be accessible to the burglar, leaving him no option. The burglar, of course, can trick you into opening the door, and so having lock security isn't always enough. You must be on guard against being pressured or talked into opening your front door. There is a good rule to follow, though. When in doubt, keep your door locked. It may later prove to be an embarrassment, but this is the lesser of two evils.

Damage to Your Home

About two-thirds of the burglaries reported in one study indicated there was no property damage; where damage did occur, the value of the amount of damage was usually fairly low. In some instances a burglar may do more damage to a door in his efforts at entry than inside the house or apartment. A burglar may resort to violence if he does not feel he is getting enough.

People who have very modest apartments or homes sometimes feel they are safe and secure since their possessions are of little value. But, as we have mentioned before, for the most part burglaries do involve modest-cost items. Burglars will go for typewriters, TV sets, costume jewelry, hi-fi components, but if these aren't available, will steal anything that isn't fastened down. The reason for this is that the burglary is being done by a nonprofessional. The professional burglar selects his victim, makes sure that the robbery is worth the risk. In some instances he may have an opportunity to visit the home or apartment and will then mentally assess all of those items having a high-market value. The nonprofessional, however, breaks in and hopes for the best. And if he can't find the best, then he takes whatever he can.

In a survey made of a particular area, the following information was obtained:

- In three cases, all residential, the premises were occupied at the time of the burglary or burglary attempt.
- Of the eight residential burglaries that occurred while the premises were unoccupied, the premises were left vacant for one hour or less in three cases.
- In two of four attempted burglaries, the potential intruder failed to gain entry because of effective preventive measures in operation.
- In only one residential burglary was there a dog on the premises at the time of the burglary.
- In two of five nonresidential burglarized sites that had alarm systems, the burglars managed to bypass the alarm.
- In six out of nine cases in which someone saw or heard the burglar, the observer was a neighbor.
- In half of fourteen cases in which the victim had an idea who committed the offense, the suspected individual was a young neighborhood resident.

The trouble with these statements is that they are generalizations. They do not hold for all parts of the nation, and may vary from one neighborhood to the next. They do have some value in that they may supply some idea of the best defense to take.

The Victims of the Offense

- Victims are more likely than nonvictims to be aware of a general crime problem in their neighborhood. Once someone becomes a victim he also becomes a concerned citizen.
- Victims of burglary are more likely to be victims of other crimes than are nonvictims of burglary. Just as there is such a thing as being accident-prone, so too is there such a thing as being "victim-prone." Some victims, after a burglary, become very security-conscious, but as the in-

cident fades into the past, they resume their former careless habits and so suffer another burglary, and then
another.

· Nonvictims are more likely to take simple precautions
against burglary than are victims. This may sound like a
contradiction, but the nonvictims are nonvictims for the
very reason that they do take precautions.

· Burglarized structures are more likely to be on corner lots.

The Burglar's Tools

We have mentioned some common tools of the burglar: the
"cheater" or "shove knife" or "shim" made of light metal or
plastic, screwdrivers, glass cutters, lock pullers, vise-grip pliers
for twisting doorknobs and wrecking the interior mechanisms,
lock picks, and fishhooks for use as lock picks.

However, because so many burglaries are now taking place
in the daytime, many burglars resort to some subterfuge for
getting into a house or apartment. In one case burglars bought
tickets to a highly popular show and mailed them to the residents of an apartment with the compliments of the theater
manager. The thieves watched the "lucky" couple as they left
their home and knew exactly how much time they had for
their burglary. In another example, burglars parked a large
crate marked "television receiver" right in front of an apartment door. One of the burglars crept into the crate and then,
unobserved, was able to saw his way in through the front
door.

Subterfuge Techniques

In one method, a man and a woman, or two women, use a
baby as a means of getting into the houses or apartments of
elderly women. They explain that the baby is hungry and
simply ask for permission to warm the baby's milk bottle. After
gaining admission, one of the two thieves goes into the kitchen

and, of course, is accompanied by the occupant. The other thief is then free to ransack the place.

The Telephone-Call Trick

Some small residence hotels and rooming houses have a single telephone for the use of occupants, generally located on a lower floor. A thief will get the names of the residents, and then telephone them from an outside corner telephone. His associate, knowing the full details of the call, is at the victim's door as soon as he leaves and forces his way in. Quite often the victim, thinking he will return in a few minutes, leaves the door unlocked. The victim is kept on the phone long enough to give the second thief enough time to sweep through the rooms to pick up anything of value.

The Inspectors

All a thief needs to do is to put on some kind of uniform and wear a cap with the word "Inspector" prominently displayed on it. He can then claim to be a wiring inspector, a sanitation inspector, a house-safety inspector, a boiler inspector, a water inspector, or any other kind of inspector. He then suggests that he be allowed to make an inspection, as required annually by the laws of the city or town. If he is denied admission, he may mumble something about the possibility of a fine for noninspection. Once inside the house he usually looks around for any item of value he can pick up.

Glossary

ALARM. To alert or warn. Can be used interchangeably to denote a particular warning device, such as a bell, horn, or siren, or a complete protection system.

ALARM DELAY CONTROL SWITCH. Switch in an alarm system that allows entry without sounding siren for specific period of time.

AMP. Abbreviation for ampere. The basic unit of electrical current.

ANGLE STRIKE. A strike in which the bolt drops vertically through the strike. See also STRIKE.

ANNUNCIATOR. Form of alarm system. Sounds a buzzer or horn when door or window is opened, but stops as soon as either one is closed again.

AREA PROTECTION. Defense of a total space; a system is said to furnish area protection when it detects and responds to an undesirable condition (such as an intruder) anywhere within the guarded space, such as an entire room.

ARMATURE. Moving section of a relay, corresponding to blade of a knife switch. Mechanical portion of a relay for opening and closing electrical circuits.

ARMOR COLLAR. Metal plate placed over lock cylinder, capable of rotating to prevent removal of cylinder by puller.

AUTOMATIC LIGHT SWITCH. Switch that operates exterior floodlights when alarm system is tripped. Also used in conjunction wth home alarm system to put on interior lights.

AUTOMATIC RESET. Device for automatic resetting of an alarm system after it has stopped ringing.

AUTOMATIC TELEPHONE DIALER. Instrument connected to an alarm system for dialing a predetermined number and playing a prerecorded message in case of intrusion.

BATTERY CHARGER. Unit for recharging alkaline or nickel-cadmium cells. When added to an alarm system that does not have an internal battery charger, will keep battery in peak operating condition.

BUNCO. General name applied to confidence schemes.

CAPACITY ALARM. Alarm that is sensitive to the presence of a moving person, or object.

CAT BURGLAR. Thief who enters occupied home or apartment at night. Considered most dangerous type and is frequently armed.

CENTRAL STATION. Specific location at which warning signals from alarm systems can be received, such as office of a detective agency, police station, or guard office in a building complex. Alarm systems that alert guards at a central station, whether via telephone lines or radio waves, are called central station alarms. If there is no audible alarm at the protected location, such systems may be called silent alarms. At the central station the alarm signal can be in the form of a flashing light on a guard panel and/or audible alarm, such as bell or buzzer.

COIN SMACK. One type of confidence game.

CON MAN. Abbreviation for confidence man. A bunco artist.

DEADBOLT. Solid piece of metal, usually in rectangular shape, but can also be round or semicircular, used in a lock so arranged that it cannot be pushed back externally but only by operation of the lock itself. Generally used in quality locks for maximum security.

DETECTOR. A sensor. A device, usually electrical, electro-mechanical, or electronic, that can respond to a specific physical condition or a change in conditions, and develop an electrical signal as a consequence of the condition or change. Often identified according to the type of physical condition to which it responds—i.e. sound detector, vibration detector.

DETERRENT. Something that hinders, discourages, or restrains a thief. The effectiveness of a security-protection system can be expressed in terms of its deterrent value. The greater the difficulty a potential intruder may have when he tries to defeat a protective device or system, the greater its deterrent value. A deadbolt lock has greater deterrent value than a spring-latch lock.

DOOR CHAIN. Connected metal links that permit limited opening of door. Comes equipped with or without locks.

DOOR CORDS. Fitted with special connection blocks, these cords are made with flexible two-conductor cable and are used to supply electrical connections to devices or equipment mounted on hinged access closures, such as doors or windows.

DOOR SWITCH. Key-operated electrical switch. Also known as key or shunt switch.

DOOR TRIP. Switch that is activated by opening a door.

DOUBLE-CYLINDER MORTISE DEADLOCK. Lock that can be keyed from inside and outside. Operates rectangular metal bolt that slides horizontally into mortised section in door jamb.

DURATION TIMER. Electronic device for switching off alarm automatically after about three or four minutes, resetting itself to sound again if the intruder should return.

ELECTRIC EYE. Photoelectric device used in alarm systems.

ELECTRIC PENCIL. An electrically operated scriber used to mark metal, plastic, wood, or glass, thus enabling owner to put personal identification on equipment such as typewriters, radios, TV sets.

ELECTRICAL SWITCH LOCK. Key-operated switch used for turning electrical circuits on and off.

EMERGENCY SWITCH. Panic button used to trip an alarm system manually. Same as panic button or panic switch.

ENTRY-DELAY SWITCH. Used to activate built-in electronic time-delay circuit. When in the "on" position, alarm sounds within seconds. This is normal position when occupants leave premises. Similar time delay permits occupants to switch system off upon returning.

FAIL-SAFE. System that alerts user in event of equipment or

circuit failure. A supervised or closed-circuit protective system is said to be fail-safe in that a cut wire, bad connection, or defective sensor will cause an alarm.

FENCE. A receiver of stolen merchandise.

FIELD. Area of coverage of an alarm device using ultrasonic, infrared, or microwaves.

FORCED ENTRY. Illegal access to a protected area by use of mechanical force.

FOX POLICE LOCK. Metal bar fitting a recessed holder in the floor and connected at the other end to a door lock.

FRONT PLATE. Metal plate used for protecting lock cylinder against a lock puller.

FRUIT. Term sometimes applied to homosexuals.

GRAND-THEFT PERSON. Police terminology for action of pickpocket.

HEIST. Theft.

HOT BURGLAR. Burglar who prefers working in same room as victim so as to keep victim under observation. See also CAT BURGLAR.

IC. Integrated circuit. Used in some types of solid-state alarm systems.

IGNITION DRY CELL. 1½-volt battery used in some alarm systems as the primary power source or as a backup standby unit.

INDICATOR LIGHT. Light that indicates an alarm system has been activated.

INFRARED. Literally, beyond red; invisible part of the light spectrum whose rays have longer wavelengths than visible red light; a high proportion of the energy emitted by heat lamps is in the infrared region. Infrared light is often used in photoelectric alarm systems. Sometimes called black light although this expression is also applied to ultraviolet light.

JAMAICAN SWITCH. One type of confidence game.

JAMAICAN TRUST GAME. A confidence game.

JAMB SPREADER. Any tool used to widen the distance between a door and its jamb.

JIGGLING. Act of opening a lock with any device that will raise the tumblers in the lock.

JIMMY. Short crowbar used by burglars to force doors and windows.

KEY-IN-KNOB LOCK. Door lock in which the key is inserted directly into the door knob. A combination knob and door lock.

KEY-SHUNT LOCK. Simple key-operated switch used to temporarily shunt or bypass a protective sensor, such as a magnetic switch used on a door or similar access closure, permitting authorized entry without triggering an alarm.

KEY SWITCH. Key-operated electrical switch. Also known as door or shunt switch.

LANTERN BATTERY. 6-volt battery available in several sizes. Used as primary power source in alarm systems or as backup standby unit.

LOCAL ALARM. An alarm situated at the protected property in contrast to one in another location; a self-contained horn or bell in alarm equipment is a local alarm, as is a bell or siren on the outside of the protected building.

LOCK ALARM. Lock that contains a built-in alarm.

LOCK MOUNT. Bracket for use in autos to prevent theft of stereo or tape units.

LOCK PICK. Various burglary tools for picking locks—that is, opening locks without keys.

LOIDING. Technique for using a shim to open a spring latch.

MAGNETIC SWITCH. A switch that has two or more reedlike metallic structures that carry electrical contacts and are magnetically sensitive. Used for door and window protection.

MARK. Intended victim.

MERCURY TILT SWITCH. Switch that closes if its position is changed.

MEXICAN CHARITY SWITCH. Type of confidence game.

MICROWAVE. Extremely high frequency radio waves; frequencies measured in hundreds of millions of cycles (Hertz) per second. At these frequencies such waves bounce back or echo from various objects. Used in some types of alarm systems.

MILLIAMP. Abbreviation for milliampere. A milliampere is a thousandth of an ampere. See AMP.

MONITOR. To watch over. An intrusion-alarm system may be said to monitor the premises. A guard may watch his monitor to maintain surveillance of an area covered by a TV camera.

MORTISE LOCK. Combination of deadbolt with a lock with spring latch.

NC. Abbreviation for normally closed. Refers to devices or circuits in which electrical contacts are kept closed under normal circumstances, opening when disturbed or activated. Window foil is one type of NC sensor, as is a magnetic switch.

NO. Abbreviation for normally open. Refers to devices or circuits in which electrical contacts are kept open under normal conditions, closing when disturbed or activated. A standard electrical switch is a NO device.

OMNIDIRECTIONAL FIELD. Invisible detection field that radiates from an alarm device. Refer to FIELD.

ON-OFF SWITCH. Switch for turning a device to its on or active position or for deactivating it—turning it off.

PADDY HUSTLE. One type of confidence game.

PANIC BUTTON. Manual switch for emergency alarm. Also known as emergency switch or panic switch.

PANIC PROOF. Device on a lock that permits instant opening. Also used with alarm systems for instant shutoff.

PENDULUM SWITCH. A switch that works as a motion sensor. Switch changes if car or part of car is moved (i.e., trunk or door or hood are opened).

PERIMETER PROTECTION. Defense of the outer edge or surface of an enclosed area; a system is said to furnish perimeter protection when it detects and responds to anyone attempting to enter the area. A fence or wall is a form of physical perimeter protection.

PHOTOELECTRIC. Refers to electricity or electrical signals produced by light. Sometimes called electric eyes, photoelectric cells (or sensors) are used in some types of intrusion-alarm systems.

PICK MEN. Burglars who specialize in opening locks using various tools as picks.

PIGEON DROP. One type of confidence game.

PLUNGER SWITCH. Switch that has a button. Used for opening or closing electrical circuits when button is depressed or released.

POINT PROTECTION. Defense of a specific object, such as file, cabinet, safe, or single door. A system offers point protection when it detects and responds to anyone interfering with or attempting to touch a guarded object.

PRE-ENTRY ALARM. Alarm system that becomes operative before break-in.

PREMISES. A site or location. May refer to a single room, a suite, an entire building, or even a tract of real estate.

PRESSURE MAT. Switch used for concealment under carpets or throw rugs at entrances, near patios, at foot of stairs.

PULL TRAP. An intrusion detector utilizing spring-loaded contacts and a removable clip and actuated by a trip cord. Used for protection of garage doors, doorways, gates, driveways, and skylights.

PUSHBUTTON LOCK. A type of combination lock opened by pushing buttons in a particular sequence. Does not require a key.

PUSH KNIFE. Special knife with flexible thin blade that can be inserted between a door jamb and door, or window frame and window. Used by burglars to release latches and certain types of locks.

RELAY. Electrically operated switch. There are two main types used in security: (1) electromagnetic relay consisting of a coil magnet, and a movable spring-restrained armature, plus two or more switch contacts; (2) solid-state relay using semiconductor devices such as transistors and silicon-controlled rectifiers (SCR's).

REMOTE ALARM. Alarm device located elsewhere than on protected premises—for example, an alarm bell that rings in the home if someone tries to enter a guest cottage elsewhere on an estate is a remote alarm. A central station alarm is one type of remote alarm.

RINGOFF. Discontinuance or cessation of alarm.

ROUND-KEY LOCK. Lock using a round key. Helpful in security since it is difficult to duplicate the key.

ROYAL SHIM. Playing card used as a shim.

SAW-PROOF BOLT. Part of lock that contains a bolt with one or more hard steel rods inside it. Rods are free to rotate. If bolt is hacksawed, rotating rods prevent further progress of hacksaw blades.

SCAM. General name applied to bunco or confidence schemes.

SECOND-STORY MAN. Burglar who prefers working in vacant part of the house, even though other parts of house may be occupied. See also HOT BURGLAR and CAT BURGLAR.

SECURITY. From the Latin, *securus*, freedom from care. Freedom from danger or fear; feeling or condition of being safe.

SENSITIVITY CONTROL. Adjustment of controlling range and sensitivity of an alarm system.

SENSOR. A device, generally electrical, electronic, or electromechanical, that responds to specific physical conditions and initiates action or develops an electrical signal relating to those conditions. See also DETECTOR.

SHELF LIFE. The useful life of a battery when unused. The period of time during which a battery will deliver electrical power before failure occurs due to chemical deterioration.

SHIM. Plastic playing card, portion of a venetian blind, or any similar thin, flexible material that can be inserted between a latch and door frame.

SHUNT SWITCH. Key-operated electrical switch. Also known as door or key switch.

SILENT ALARM. System that does not produce audible alarm but sends a signal to a central station.

SINGLE-CYLINDER MORTISE DEADLOCK. Lock that can be keyed from the outside only. Operates rectangular metal bolt that slides horizontally into mortised section in door jamb.

SLAM PULLER. Burglary tool used for opening car trunks or doors.

SLIDE SWITCH. Type of switch opened or closed by a sliding control. Used as on/off switch for alarm system or as an exit/entry alarm switch.

SNATCHER. Thief who specializes in purse snatching.

SOLID STATE. Electronic circuit containing devices such as transistors and crystal diodes.

SPRING LATCH. Easily opened lock with bevel-edged bolt. Usually manufactured to coarse tolerances.

SPST SWITCH. Single-pole single-throw switch. Simple on-off switch used in some alarm systems.

STRIKE. Part of lock into which the bolt fits when the door is locked.

SWITCH MAT. Switch placed under a mat or rug. Used for hallway and stair protection. Also called pressure mat.

TAMPER SWITCH. Electrical switch used to actuate an alarm in any attempt to manipulate or modify a piece of equipment. Often used in intrusion-detection systems to prevent anyone from gaining access to the circuitry or changing the sensitivity or operating characteristics of the equipment. Generally a plunger type or magnetic switch mounted within the equipment's enclosure.

TEST BUTTON. Switch used for momentary testing of an alarm system.

TILL TAP. One type of confidence game.

TILT DETECTOR. Sensor that is sensitive to a change in position.

TIMED RINGOFF. Amount of time an alarm will stay off before being automatically reactivated.

TRANSDUCER. Device for changing one form of energy to another. An alarm is a transducer—it changes electrical energy to sound energy.

TRAP ZONE. Area protected by an alarm system using a wave technique, such as an ultrasonic alarm.

TRIP CORD. An almost invisible or hidden string, cord, or wire arranged in such a way that it will be disturbed by an intruder. Generally used with a pull trap.

ULTRASONIC. Literally, "beyond that which can be heard." Physical vibrations at frequencies beyond the range of human hearing, or generally above twenty thousand cycles per second (Hertz). The so-called silent dog whistle produces ultrasonic signals and ultrasonic vibrations are used in some types of intrusion-alarm systems for motion detection.

V. Abbreviation for volts or voltage. The volt is the basic unit of electrical pressure.

VIBRATION SENSOR. Electromechanical device used to detect mechanical vibrations such as those caused by someone jimmying a door or window or walking across a room. Some types employ a spring pendulum.

VIEWER. Peephole device mounted in door so occupant can see visitors without opening door.

VIN. Vehicle identification number.

VOLTAGE-SURGE SENSOR. Sensor that will keep an alarm system from activating if the line voltage increases momentarily or surges. Eliminates false triggering.

WALL PENETRATION. Ability of radiated field from alarm device to pass through a wall. Wall penetration is not achieved by ultrasonic or infrared alarm systems. Radio waves do go through walls but penetration is determined by type of radio wave system used and amount of metal in wall.

WALL SENSOR. Sensor attached to wall. Touch of intruder's hand breaks a magnetic contact that sends a radio impulse to a master control unit and triggers the alarm.

WARNING DEVICE. Electrical, electromechanical, mechanical, or chemical component used to call attention to a specific condition. May be audible, as an alarm bell, buzzer, horn, or siren; may be visual as a flashing light; may even be odoriferous, in the cases of special substances added to otherwise odorless, but poisonous gases, to warn someone of a leak.

WHEEL LOCK. Used for protecting costly custom "Mag" and standard wheels against theft. Replaces one lug nut on each wheel.

WINDOW-FOIL SENSOR. Strip of narrow, metallic foil cemented around a window and forming a continuous conductive path that can be part of an electrical circuit. Detects glass breakage.